The Timucua Indians

U P F

Young Readers Library

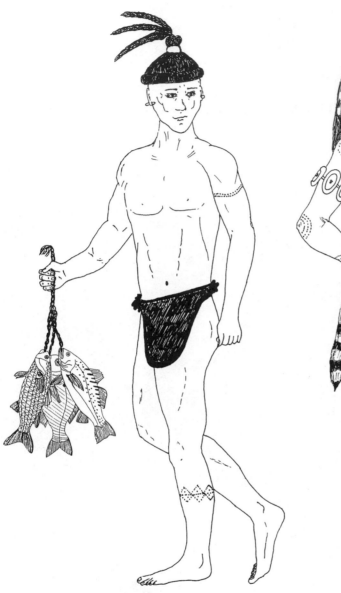

University Press of Florida

Gainesville · Tallahassee · Tampa · Boca Raton

Pensacola · Orlando · Miami · Jacksonville

The Timucua Indians

A Native American Detective Story

Kelley G. Weitzel

Illustrations by
Kelley G. Weitzel,
Heather Shuke, and
Rachelle Marker

05   04   03   02   6   5   4   3   2

Library of Congress Cataloging-in-Publication Data
Weitzel, Kelley G., 1969–
The Timucua Indians: a Native American detective story / Kelley
G. Weitzel; illustrations by Kelley G. Weitzel, Heather Shuke, and
Rachelle Marker.
p. cm. — (UPF young readers library)
Includes bibliographical references and index.
Summary: Discusses the history, language, customs, and daily life of
the Timucua Indians who lived in northern Florida and southern
Georgia. Includes activities to reinforce information presented.
ISBN 0-8130-1738-6 (p: alk. paper)
1. Timucua Indians Juvenile literature. [1. Timucua Indians. 2. Indi-
ans of North America—Florida. 3. Indians of North America—
Georgia.] I. Series.
E99.T55W45   2000
975.004'973—dc21   99-23749

The University Press of Florida is the scholarly publishing agency
for the State University System of Florida, comprising Florida
A&M University, Florida Atlantic University, Florida International
University, Florida State University, University of Central Florida,
University of Florida, University of North Florida, University of
South Florida, and University of West Florida.

University Press of Florida
15 Northwest 15th Street
Gainesville, FL 32611
http://www.upf.com

This book is dedicated to the Timucua children,
who lived long ago. Let's live a lifetime for them.

Contents

Preface

The Timucua Indians: A Native American Detective Story is written for kids. It's fun, and it's true, so teachers can use it to make a classroom study that everyone will enjoy.

I wrote this book to make sure that we never forget about the Timucua people. They were people, just like us. They lived right here in North Florida where I grew up. They looked up at the same stars. They ate the same wild blackberries that grow by my fence. They played games and got into arguments and sang songs. They were real people—just like you! When you walk in the woods, try to imagine that you are a Timucua. It will help you remember them forever.

Many people have helped to make this book a good one. Jerald Milanich critiqued it to make sure all of the facts about the Timucua were correct and even recommended it to his own publisher. My staff at the E. Dale Joyner Nature Preserve at Pelotes Island aided in fact-finding and creating artwork. These intrepid preserve naturalists (past and present) include Tammy Cooper, Christina Zabinski, Rachelle Marker, and Heather Shuke. My sister and friend, Kimber Herrera, held my hand through the long series of rejection letters preceding a fruitful relationship with the University Press of Florida. And finally, for offering a level head, a keen ear, and loving support, my thanks and love go to Sheldon Pantin.

Timeline

When Did Important Things Happen?

15,000 years ago	Paleoindians cross the Bering land bridge into North America.
13,000 years ago	Paleoindians get to Florida.
2,500 years ago	The Native Americans in North Florida and South Georgia settle down into villages. They are called Timucua Indians today.
500 + years ago	Columbus lands in the West Indies and "discovers" the Americas.
400 + years ago	The French and Spanish build forts and missions in Florida. The Timucua culture is still healthy.
230 + years ago	The last Timucua Indian dies in Cuba.
Today (2000 A.D.)	A cool kids' book is written about the Timucua.

Introduction

What Is a Detective Directive?

detective   (dee-TEK-tiv) 1. a person who discovers the truth. 2. an investigator.

directive   (di-REK-tiv) 1. a task to accomplish. 2. an order or challenge.

archaeologist   (ar-kee-OL-oh-jist) 1. a person who investigates things (like tools and pottery) that were left behind by people who lived long ago.

Being an archaeologist is a little like being a detective. When archaeologists find a skeleton, part of a pot, or a broken projectile (arrow) point, they only have clues to what happened long ago. They have to put these clues together to discover the truth about the past.

Learning about the Timucua Indians is a true challenge. We can't ask them any questions, because they are gone forever. We have to look at old pictures, old stories, and old things these Native Americans left behind.

It is up to us to discover the truth about the Timucua.

 In each chapter of this book, you will see *Detective Directives*. They will ask you to use your "detective mind" to figure out what is true about the Timucua and what is not. If you need help, the answers are in the back. You can find the words in **bold text** in a dictionary in the back, too. This dictionary is called a "glossary."

How do you pronounce the strange, new words in this book? Look for something like this: (ar-kee-OL-oh-jist). This tells you how to sound out the word. The SMALL CAPITAL LETTERS tell you which part of the word to say the loudest. Try this word: hamburger. You say HAM-bur-gur, because the first part is the loudest. You don't say (ham-BUR-gur) or (ham-bur-GUR).

☞ Cool Fact: To say "hamburger" in Spanish, you say *hamburguesa*. It is pronounced (um-bur-GE-sa). Now you'll be able to pronounce (say) all the strange words in this book.

☞ You are about to begin a journey that will take you 15,000 years into the past. You'll see alligator hunts and great battles, learn some of the Timucua language, meet a Timucua chief, and investigate ancient Native American artifacts. Detective, let your **quest** for the truth begin!

1

Prehistory

How Did People Live Way Back Then?

WHAT IS HISTORY? History is anything that has happened in the past. It can be about kings and chiefs, faraway countries, or even the story of how your grandmother learned to make spaghetti. It can be yesterday or 10,000 years ago.

WHAT IS PREHISTORY? "Pre" means "before." In this case, it means "before people wrote down their history." Before people could write, they kept their history by telling stories. After all, "story" is a big part HISTORY. Sometimes grandparents told the same stories every night so that their grandchildren would remember. Other times a special person was the storyteller for the whole village. Remembering and telling all the village stories was a big job. If something happened to the storyteller, the village history could be lost forever.

Many true stories about the Timucua Indians have been forgotten. Because so few of the Timucua ever learned to read and write, hardly any of their stories were written down. Now all of the Timucua are gone, so we have to work hard to find out what these people were like.

When **Europeans** sailed across the Atlantic Ocean to America, they met the Timucua people. Many of these Europeans wrote down stories about the Timucua. Some stories were true, and some stories were not. Studying history takes detective work. It is up to us to find the truest stories and remember them.

> **Europeans are people from Spain, France, England, and other countries in Europe.**

Detective Directive 1: Why is it important to write down history? When you tell a story over and over without writing it down, the story always changes. Try this activity with at least three helpers. If you try it at school during lunchtime with lots of people, it works even better. Say this sentence to helper #1. The others should not be listening.

"My cousin, Karen, cares for horses, elephants, hens, earthworms, hawks, and eagles. She's a zany 27-year-old zoologist at the Jacksonville Zoo."

You can say it for helper #1 a few times, but after that, don't remind her again. Now, she has to say it to helper #2. After that, helper #2 tells the next person. Keep going down the line. Be sure to whisper, so no one else can hear the sentences ahead of time. The last helper should say the sentences back to you. On the lines below, write down what the last helper says.

_____

_____

_____

_____

How much has the story changed? Did the last helper leave out some animals or describing words? _____ If you don't write down history, it changes with each person who tells it. The final story might be totally different from the one you started with!

WHERE DID NATIVE AMERICANS COME FROM? The people who were here 15,000 years ago were called Paleoindians (PAY-lee-oh-Indians).

> **Siberia is in northern Russia.**

> **A glacier is a giant sheet of ice that is a mile thick.**

They walked to many places. In fact, they walked all the way across **Siberia.** Today, when you get to the northeastern edge of Siberia, you run into the Pacific Ocean. But around 15,000 years ago, the planet was in an Ice Age. That means that a lot of the water in the oceans was frozen into **glaciers.**

Since so much water was frozen, there wasn't as much water left in the ocean. In some places, the bottom of the ocean was completely dry. One of those places was by Siberia. The Paleoindians walked right across this dry ocean bottom. Their path is called the Bering land bridge, and it took them right into Alaska. Today the land bridge is mostly covered by the ocean again. It is cold in Alaska today, and it was cold then, too.

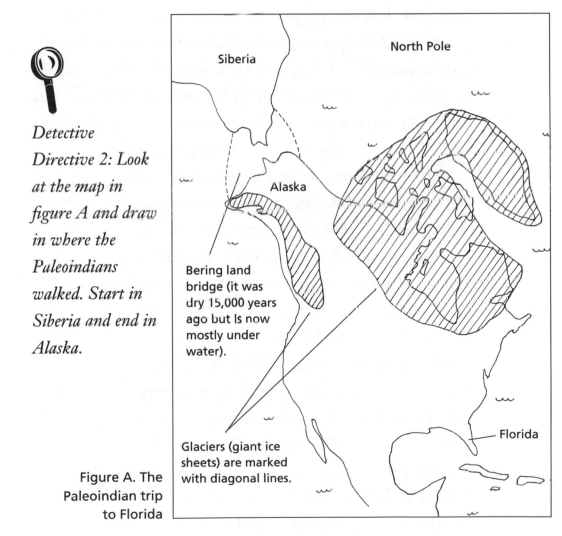

Detective Directive 2: Look at the map in figure A and draw in where the Paleoindians walked. Start in Siberia and end in Alaska.

North Pole

Siberia

Alaska

Bering land bridge (it was dry 15,000 years ago but is now mostly under water).

Glaciers (giant ice sheets) are marked with diagonal lines.

Florida

Figure A. The Paleoindian trip to Florida

These Paleoindians hunted huge nomadic animals like mastodons (large hairy elephants), giant bison (buffalo), camels, and whales. After they got to Alaska, they kept on walking, following the herds of large animals. Some walked through Mexico all the way to the tip of South America. Others stayed at different places in the United States. The Paleoindians may have gotten to Florida about 13,000 years ago. The ones who stayed in North Florida would later be called the Timucua people.

Before 2,500 years ago, the Native Americans in North Florida and South Georgia did not live in the same place all the time. They moved around to follow herds of animals, to find fresh water, and to look for ripe fruits and vegetables. They did not use bows and arrows or grow gardens.

Around 2,500 years ago, their lives started to change. Native Americans learned to use the bow and arrow. This change made them better hunters, so they didn't have to travel so much to find meat. They also learned to grow corn and beans in gardens so they could get enough plant food for many people. Now that they had more food, larger groups of people settled down together into villages. They could also stay in one place for longer periods of time. Because their life-style changed, their **culture**, or way of life, also changed. This new culture, and the people who lived it, are called Timucua by historians today.

The Paleoindians who stayed in other parts of the United States grew into hundreds of other native groups, like the Arapaho, Cherokee, and Navajo.

Detective Directive 3: Look at the map in figure A again. Draw in a path that the Paleoindians may have taken to get from Alaska to Florida. (Hint: Glaciers are too cold to walk on.)

WHY ARE ALL THE NATIVE AMERICAN TRIBES DIFFERENT? People who live in different places live in different ways. If you live where it is very cold, as it is in Alaska, you may live in an igloo and go ice fishing. If you live in a warm place with good soil, you may live in a hut and plant a huge garden. If you live on the grassy plains, you may live in a teepee and hunt buffalo. The Paleoindians learned to live in many different places. That's why there are so many different kinds of Native Americans today. Each Native American group has its own religion, foods, dances, laws, clothing, and homes.

WHY WERE NATIVE AMERICANS CALLED "INDIANS"? When Christopher Columbus "sailed the ocean blue in fourteen hundred-ninety-two," he didn't know that the Americas were out there across the ocean. No one did. He planned to sail around the world to get to **Indonesia.** (That's a group of islands near China.) No one had ever done it before, and there was no map to show him the way. When Columbus got close to North America, he thought he was almost to the East Indies, so he called all the people he saw "Indians." Oops!

> Indonesia is also called the "East Indies" or the "Spice Islands."

"Native American" means "people who were here first." The reason we still say "Timucua Indians" is because the Timucua are all gone. Not a single Timucua is alive today. It is polite and correct to say "Native American" instead of "Indian" for tribes that are still here today.

Today these islands around Cuba are called the West Indies, since Columbus thought they were the East Indies.

Detective Directive 4: Look at figure B. The arrow shows where Columbus wanted to go. You can't see the East Indies, because they're on the other side of the world from us. Columbus never made it to the East Indies. Draw where Columbus really went. Start in Spain and end in the West Indies. Exploring is a lot harder than it looks!

Figure B. Columbus's journey

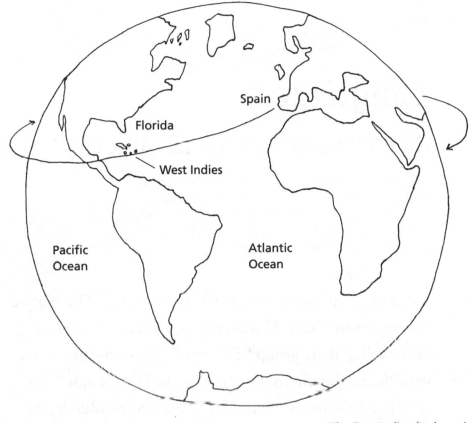

The arrow shows where Columbus wanted to go. He didn't know that North and South America were in the way.

The East Indies (Indonesia) are a group of islands known for their food spices. They are south of China and north of Australia.

2

Language

Can You Learn to Speak Timucua?

WHERE DID THE NAME "TIMUCUA" COME FROM? The Native Americans in North Florida and South Georgia probably never called their group "Timucua" (Ti-MOO-qua). They used names for themselves that meant "the people." So, where did the name "Timucua" come from? Here's one idea. Chief Saturiwa (Sa-chur-EE-wa) told the French that he had captured a piece of silver from Thimogona (Tee-ma-GO-na). He said that Thimogona lived across the river. "Thimogona" probably meant "enemy." Chief Saturiwa's greatest enemy, Outina, lived right on the other side of the St. Johns River.

We think the French soldiers started using the name "Thimogona" to mean *all* of the Native Americans in North Florida and South Georgia, not just the ones across the river. These are some of the different ways the French and Spanish spelled this name: Thimogona, Thimogoa, Timoga, Timucua. Even when you do write down histories, you have to be sure of your spelling. There is no way to go back 400 years to check it out.

Detective Directive 5: Say the following names out loud. Do you think the name "Timucua" came from "Thimogona"?

(1) Thimogona (Tee-mo-GO-na)

(2) Thimogoa (Tee-mo-GO-a)

(3) Timoga (Tee-MO-ga)

(4) Timucua (Tee-MOO-kwa)

Lots of people argue over how to pronounce the name "Timucua." Since these Native Americans didn't use that word themselves, there was never a correct Timucua way to say it. The Spanish would have said Tee-MOO-kwa. Other people say Ti-MOO-kwa or Timucuan (TI-muh-kwan). It's up to you. Today, when we say "Timucua," we mean all the Native Americans in North Florida and South Georgia who spoke the same language. We call this language "Timucua." After all, in Germany they speak German, and in England they speak English. On Timucua lands, they spoke Timucua.

Detective Directive 6: Look on the map of Florida and Georgia in figure C. Color the places where the Timucua lived. What were the names of some other Native American groups who lived in Florida and Georgia? Write their names here.

_____

_____

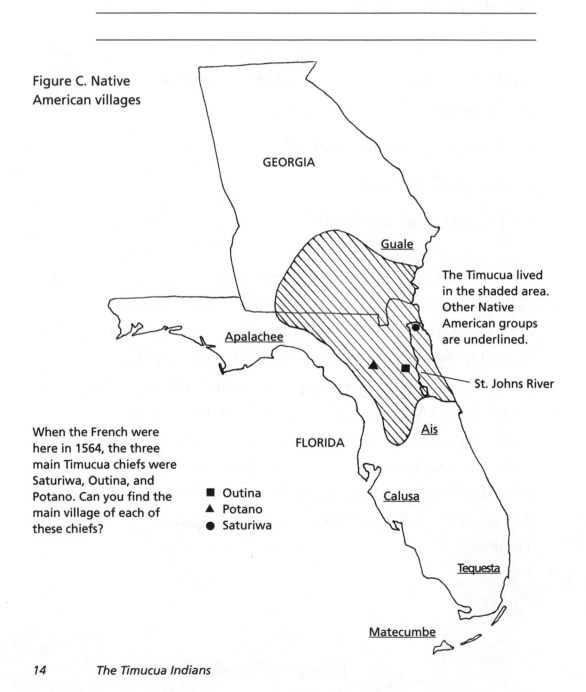

Figure C. Native American villages

GEORGIA

Guale

The Timucua lived in the shaded area. Other Native American groups are underlined.

Apalachee

St. Johns River

When the French were here in 1564, the three main Timucua chiefs were Saturiwa, Outina, and Potano. Can you find the main village of each of these chiefs?

Ais

FLORIDA

■ Outina
▲ Potano
● Saturiwa

Calusa

Tequesta

Matecumbe

Detective Directive 7: Look at figure D. It has the names of some cities that are in Florida and Georgia today. Now look back at figure C. Figure C shows where the different Native American groups lived long ago. By looking at both figures C and D, can you tell which groups of Native Americans lived where the cities are today? Fill in the answers below.

Jacksonville

_____

Key West

_____

Miami

_____

Orlando

_____

Savannah

_____

Tallahassee

_____

Tampa

_____

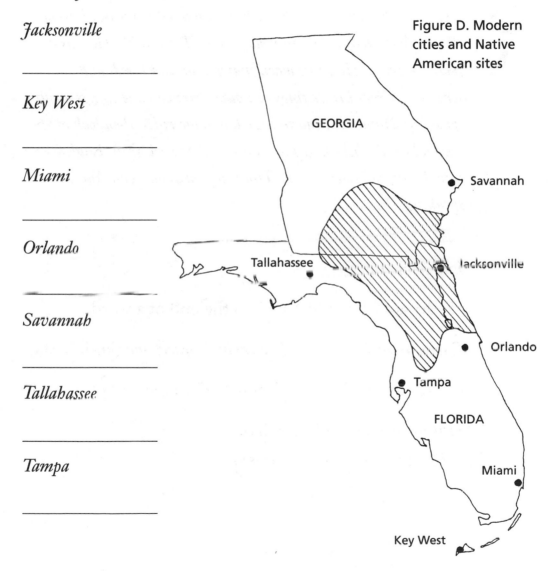

Figure D. Modern cities and Native American sites

☞ Cool Fact: The city of Tampa gets its name from a Calusa village: Tanpa. The Calusa were a powerful native group in south-central Florida. They were different from the Timucua.

Detective Directive 8: A Spanish man named Francisco Pareja (Pa-RE-ha) taught the Timucua about Christianity. He was a friar, or priest. He wrote down many Timucua words and sentences. From his writings, we have learned some things about speaking Timucua. Read the two language rules, then look at the vocabulary list below. Try to translate the words from English into Timucua. Then say the Timucua words out loud. You're speaking Timucua!

Language rules:

(1) To say "the" add "-ma" to the end of a word.

Rabbit = quelo (ke-LO). *The rabbit = quelo-ma* (ke-loh-MA)

(2) To say "his" or "her," add "-si" to the end of a word.

Hut (or house) = paha (PA-ha).
   Her hut = paha-si (pa-ha-SEE)

Vocabulary list	Change English to Timucua here.
arrow = *atulu* (ah-TOO-loo)	*(1) son* _____
canoe = *tico* (TEE-ko)	*(2) deer* _____
clan = *hasomi* (ha-SO-me)	*(3) the deer* _____
corn = *tapola* (ta-PO-la)	*(4) the corn* _____
deer = *honoso* (ho-NO-so)	*(5) the canoe* _____
his or her = *-si*	*(6) her canoe* _____
I am = *hontala* (HONE-ta-la)	*(7) his clan* _____
son = *chiri* (chee-REE)	*(8) his arrow* _____
tall = *ihiriba* (ee-hee-REE-ba)	*(9) I am tall.* _____
the = *-ma*	*(10) I am his son.* _____

☞ Cool Fact: Look at numbers 9 and 10. We think
this is how the Timucua made their sentences,
but we're not sure. Since all the Timucua are
gone, do you think we'll ever be sure? _____

HOW DID THE TIMUCUA LEARN TO READ AND WRITE? The
Timucua language was a spoken language. That means that
the Timucua did not read and write. That doesn't mean
they weren't smart enough. It just means that no one had
ever taught them to do it.

When the Spanish missionaries came to Florida, their job was to teach the Timucua about Christianity. To do this, they also had to teach them to read so that they could study the Bible.

Francisco Pareja taught many Timucua to read and write their own language. Today, we even have two letters written by Timucua people.

A Spanish friar named Luis Geronimo de Oré wrote some things about the Timucua in 1616 A.D. That's almost 400 years ago! Since this priest was Spanish, do you think he wrote this story in English? _____ No, he didn't. This story had to be translated into English by another friar, named Maynard Geiger.

This is what the English **translation** said about the Timucua: "with ease—using Pareja's books—many Indians have learned to read in less than six months and write letters to one another in their own language." (See the two books listed near the end of this chapter.)

According to Oré, it sounds like the Timucua learned to read and write fast; they were just as smart as anyone else.

Try to pronounce the name Luis Geronimo de Oré. Say it out loud five times until you think you've got it right.

Here's the Spanish way to say it: "Loo-EES Heh-RO-nee-mo de O-REH." Sound out the Spanish way and say it out loud.

Did it sound the same as what you said before? _____
Unless you've studied Spanish, you probably said something
more like this: "Loo-is Je-ro-ni-mo de Or." Can you see
how easy it would have been for the Spanish and French to
mix up the Timucua name (Thimogona—Timogoa—
Timucua)? _____

When I told you about the Timucua writing their own
letters, I got the information from someone else. When you
use someone else's ideas in your school paper, or in a book
you're writing, you have to give them credit. After all, they
did the work first. Grown-ups give credit to each other by
writing down all the information about the person or book
they learned from. Here's an example:

Oré, Fr. Luis Geronimo de, OFM. 1616. *The Martyrs of Florida (1513–
1616)*. Edited and translated by Fr. Maynard Geiger, OFM.
Franciscan Studies 18. Paterson, N.J., 1936.

We should also give credit to another book, since I found
the story there:

Granberry, Julian. *A Grammar and Dictionary of the Timucua Language.*
Tuscaloosa: University of Alabama Press, 1993.

At the end of this book, in the section called "Further
Reading for Adults," I listed all of the books I used when I
was studying about the Timucua. By giving credit to these
books, I made sure that you and your parents can learn
more about the Timucua. There's also a section called

"Cool Ways for Kids to Learn about Native Americans." It lists some good books and lots of great museums and parks to visit on the weekends. Don't forget to check it out!

True historical detectives check out the facts for themselves. Don't *just* read the books; go *talk* to the people who wrote the books. Don't *just* watch history shows on television; **interview** some people who really remember the old days. Don't *just* surf the Internet; *explore* the museums and parks you learn about. Be a real historical detective!

3

Clothes and Decorations

What Did the Timucua Look Like?

WHAT DID THE TIMUCUA LOOK LIKE? They looked very much like people today. Their skin was probably a light brown color, and they got dark suntans from being outside all day. Their hair was very dark brown or black. The Timucua, like many Native American peoples, didn't have much hair on their faces or bodies. So the men would not have had beards or hairy arms and chests. They were fairly tall, usually between five and a half and six and a half feet. The French wrote stories saying the Timucua were giants, but . . .

Detective Directive 9: Most of the Timucua skeletons that have been measured show that the men were less than six and a half feet tall. The women were a little shorter. Look at figure E. It shows how tall the Timucua

and the French were. Why do you think the French felt that the
Timucua were giants?

_____

_____

_____

Figure E. French drawing showing Timucua,
French people, and the French monument

Height in feet

HOW DID THE TIMUCUA MEN DRESS? They didn't wear as many clothes as most Floridians do today. Here are some reasons why. First, it is *hot* in Florida, and there wasn't any air conditioning back then. They didn't need to wear many clothes to keep warm. Also, the Timucua usually lived near rivers, marshes, or the ocean, so they spent a lot of time in the water, fishing, canoeing, and gathering oysters. The men wore something like a bathing suit all the time. It was called a loincloth and was made of animal skin. They didn't need much animal skin to make one, because a bathing suit is fairly small. But if they tried to make a whole suit of clothes, they would have to hunt and kill several deer. Then they would have to **cure** the hides, which takes a lot of time and effort, and would have to sew the hides together. After they put it on, they would sweat all the time, because leather keeps you really warm.

> Today some people make coats out of leather because animal skin can keep you warm.

A full set of **leather** clothes would mean too much work and too much sweat. Just wearing a loincloth is sounding better and better!

HOW DID THE WOMEN DRESS? Timucua women wore something like the bottom of a girl's bathing suit. It was probably made of animal skin. They also made a rough gray cloth from **Spanish moss**, which they wrapped around their hips or draped it from one shoulder across to the other hip.

Spanish moss is a gray, curly plant that grows in trees. Red bugs, or chiggers, live in moss. If you play with moss, the red bugs will get on you and make you itch.

They probably boiled the moss to kill the red bugs, ticks, and other tiny creatures that might live in it. Or maybe they put it near a really smoky fire, because bugs don't like smoke. Today, we have different ways to clean cotton plants before we make them into clothes, but we still have to do it.

WHAT DID THE TIMUCUA WEAR DURING COLD WEATHER? A loincloth and a moss wrap wouldn't keep anyone warm in the winter, so they had cold-weather clothes, too. They sewed leggings to keep their legs warm. Timucua leggings are pants with no seat. (Today some girls wear pants called leggings. They look like thick tights. Timucua leggings were very different.) Although the Timucua usually went barefoot, they could sew moccasins to keep their feet warm and to protect them on long trips. They wore matchcoats, too. A matchcoat is a jacket with no armholes or sleeves. You wrap it around yourself like a giant towel to keep warm. These matchcoats were made of animal skin or feathers. A coat made of feathers would really keep the wind and rain off.

WHAT DID THE KIDS WEAR? The French and Spanish didn't write much about the kids. But we do know that babies usually went naked. After all, no one sold diapers back then.

Older boys dressed like men, and older girls dressed like women.

Detective Directive 10: Look at figure F. Color the man's loincloth a very light brown, almost white. Color the woman's bottoms light brown, almost white. Color her moss cloth gray. Color the matchcoat any color you like. Sometimes the Timucua painted animal pictures on their matchcoats. You can color decorations on the matchcoat, too. To find out how to color the skin of the Timucua, look back at chapter 3 on clothes and decorations.

Figure F. Timucua clothes.

Chief Saturiwa

Timucua woman with baby

HOW DID THE TIMUCUA WEAR THEIR HAIR? They didn't cut their hair unless they wanted to show that they were very sad. If a woman's husband died, she cut her hair very short to show her sadness. Some Timucua did the same thing when a chief died. In the pictures that the French drew, none of the women braided or decorated their hair.

Detective Directive 11: Look at all of the girls in your classroom. Do any of them have their hair braided? _____ If you said "no," does that mean that girls never braid their hair? _____ Why not? (Hint: What about the girls in other classrooms, in other schools, on other days?) _____

_____

_____

The French didn't draw any Timucua women with decorated hair. Does that mean for sure that none of the Timucua women braided or decorated their hair? _____ Why not? (Hint: What about the Timucua girls living in other villages?)

_____

_____

The French drawings did show the Timucua men with decorations in their hair. Feathers and raccoon tails were two popular decorations. Sometimes a Timucua man wore all of his long hair in a ponytail on top of his head. This made him look even taller than he really was. A Timucua man could also wear his hair tied into a bun, or knot, on top of his head. This kept his hair neat and away from his eyes. The French also wrote that men carried arrows stuck into their hair knots. This may have kept the arrows dry when the men swam across a river.

Detective Directive 12: Look at figure F again. Color the woman's hair black. Her hair reaches down to her hips because she never cuts it. How long is your hair? _____ How far does it reach down your back? _____

_____

Draw two arrows sticking sideways out of the man's hair. Now color his hair black. Timucua boys—not girls—were the ones who usually decorated their hair. In Florida today, who usually wears more hair decorations, boys or girls? _____ Different cultures like different things. Each culture, or group of people, has its own jewelry, clothes, dances, houses, religions, jobs, and foods. That's what makes each culture special.

WHAT KINDS OF JEWELRY DID THEY WEAR?
Timucua men and women wore ear pins in both ears. These are like pierced earrings, but they are not shaped like rings. These pins could be made of bone, shell, pearls, or copper. (Look ahead to figure R on page 83.) Ear pins could be decorated with tiny carved pictures or colored **dyes.** French explorers wrote that the Timucua made ear decorations out of **fish bladders.** The French said that fish-

> **Dye is a paint made of berries.**

> **A fish bladder is an air sac inside the fish that helps it float under water.**

bladder ear decorations were beautiful, like **rubies.** But since fish bladders don't last in the ground for 400 years like bone ear pins do, we haven't been able to find any. We're not sure if the French stories of fish-bladder ear decorations are true or not.

The Timucua wore other kinds of jewelry, too. They made beads for necklaces and bracelets. These beads could be made of bone, shell, wood, or even pearls. They also wore jangles. These are pieces of shell, wood, or copper that dangle down from a belt or armband and jingle while you walk. Jingle + Dangle = Jangle.

The Timucua men had another kind of jewelry, called a gorget (GOR-jet). This was a big circle made of shell or copper. It might have designs carved into it. It hung from a cord around the man's neck and rested on his chest. The gorget could be used as jewelry or as protective armor. The Timucua got copper by trading with Native Americans in the mountains near what is North Carolina today.

Detective Directive 13: Look at the pictures in figure G. How could the gorget protect this man from an enemy's arrows?

_____

_____

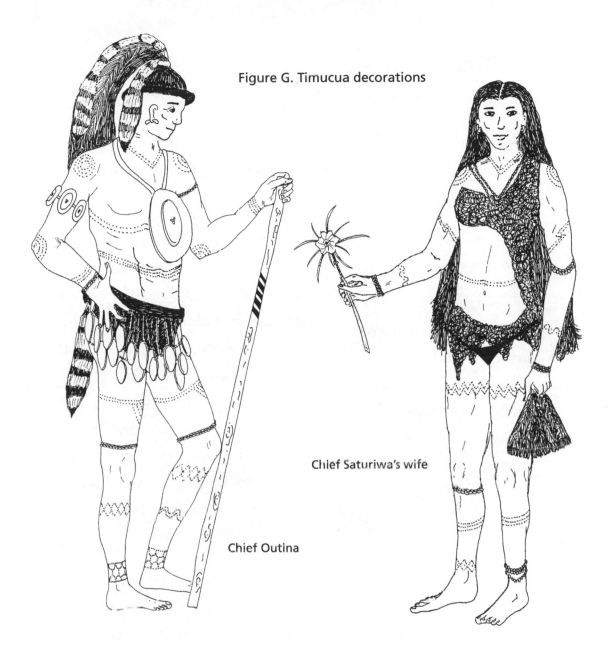

Figure G. Timucua decorations

Chief Saturiwa's wife

Chief Outina

Detective Directive 14: When the Timucua were in the woods hunting or gathering grapes, do you think they wanted to be jingling and getting their beads caught on branches? _____ Do your parents wear nice jewelry when they do yard work? _____

Do you think the Timucua wore all of their jewelry every day or just on special occasions? _____

 Detective Directive 15: Look at the pictures in figure G again. Color the beads green, the ear pins red, the jangles blue, and the gorget gray.

HOW DID THE TIMUCUA DECORATE THEIR SKIN? They really liked **tattoos.** The tattoos they put on their skin were designs made with dots. They made these dots by poking their skin with something sharp, like a shark's tooth or a bone needle. Then they would rub wood ashes mixed with berry juice into the tiny holes. Sometimes they got sick from getting tattoos. It's not very healthy to poke holes in your skin, but tattoos were important to the Timucua.

> A tattoo is a permanent mark put on the skin with needles. Getting a tattoo is a serious grown-up decision, because once it goes on it doesn't wipe off.

Girls and boys could get tattoos once they started to take on grown-up **responsibilities.** They probably earned tattoos through strength and bravery. If you had lots of tattoos, it showed your popularity and high **status**. The chief and the chief's family had more tattoos than anyone else. You could always tell who the most important people in the village were, because they had thin blue lines around their lips. These may have been tattoos or just blue paint.

Some Spanish papers say the Timucua used paint on their skin along with the tattoos.

Detective Directive 16: Look at the people in figure H. Who is the chief? Who is the chief's wife? Circle these two people. How did you know which people to choose?

_____

_____

Figure H. The chief's family and other Timucua people

4

Families and Clans

What about Timucua Moms and Dads?

HOW DID THE FAMILY ACT? We don't know that much about the Timucua family. We do know that the mother, father, and children lived in the same hut, and maybe the grandparents did, too.

The Timucua were a **matrilineal** (ma-tri-LIN-ee-al) society. "Matrilineal" means "mother line." The first part of the word, "matri," means "mother." The second part, "lineal," means "line." Your line tells you who your closest relatives are. It helps you to figure out who would be in your Timucua **clan.** The Timucua traced their "line," by going back to their mothers, grandmothers, great-grandmothers, and even great-great-grandmothers.

> A clan is made up of close relatives.

WHAT IS A NATIVE AMERICAN CLAN? Different people all over the world have different types of clans. A clan is usually made up of close relatives: cousins, aunts and uncles, grandparents, and more. Because the Timucua were matrilineal, they traced their clan through their mothers. Each person belonged to a clan. Chiefs always belonged to the Deer Clan. Some other clans were the Earth Clan and the Fish Clan. It was probably against the rules to marry someone inside your own clan, because it would be like marrying your cousin. Your mother and almost everyone blood-related to her would be in your clan. Since your parents are not blood-related to each other, your dad and his relatives would NOT be in your clan.

Does this sound confusing? Even today, we get confused when we try to figure out if someone is a first cousin once removed or a second cousin. Just remember, almost anyone who is blood-related to your mom would be in your clan.

Detective Directive 17: Let's try to figure out who would be in your Timucua clan. Look at figure I. Find the legend and answer these questions.

(1) What are the circles? _____

_____

(2) What are the triangles? _____

_____

(3) What does an = sign mean? _____

_____

(4) Who is on the top of a line going up and down? _____

_____

(5) Who is on the bottom of a line going up and down? _____

_____

(6) This is a bridge: ⊓ *What does it mean?* _____

_____

Remember, "matrilineal" means "mother line." In figure I, you'll be tracing lines through mothers to find your clan.

You are in the Earth Clan. Your goal is to find out which people would be in your Timucua clan and color their shapes green. First, find "you"—the colored square. Now, go to the top and find your great-grandmother, in a crisscross circle. She's the oldest mother, so we'll start the clan with her. Here are three rules to help you figure out who would be in your clan.

(A) Children are always in their mother's clan (not their father's). Mothers and fathers are never in the same clan.

(B) To find out who would be in your clan, start at the top and go down a line, across a line, and down a line. This helps you go from mothers down to children and across to brothers and sisters. Remember, "down, across, down."

(C) The = sign means married. When looking for your clan, never go all the way across to the other side of an = sign. This is because people can't get married if they're in the same clan. So you know the person on the other side of the = sign would not be in your clan. (Instead, look below the = sign for their children. They could be in your clan.)

Now you're ready to investigate. Who would be in your Timucua clan?

(7) Start with your great-grandmother. She would be in your clan. Color her circle green. She is married to your great-grand-father. Would he be in your clan? (Hint: See rule C.) _____ Why not? _____

_____

From the married =, go down, across, and down to your great-uncle. Would he be in your clan? (Hint: See rule B.) _____ If yes, color his triangle green.

(8) Start again with your great-grandmother. Go down, across, and down to grandmother #2. Would she be in your clan? _____ If yes,

Figure I. Timucua clans

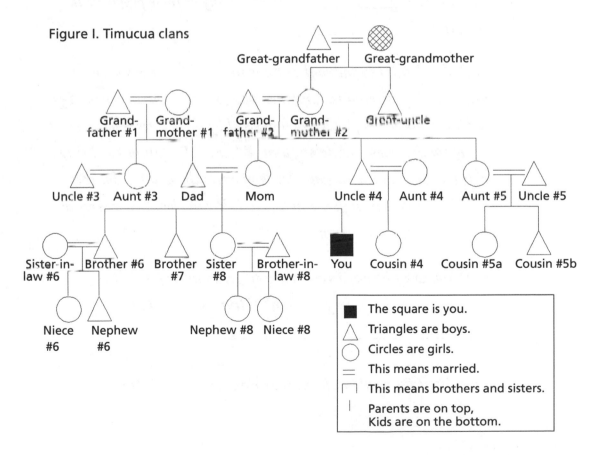

color her circle green. Your great-uncle and your grandmother would be in your clan because they are blood-related to your great-grandmother. You find blood relatives by going down, across, down.

(9) Would grandfather #2 be in your clan? _____
Why not? (Hint: See rule C.)

_____

(10) Look at grandfather #1, grandmother #1, dad, aunt #3, and uncle #3. The only way they are connected to you is by an = sign, when your father and mother got married. Can you cross to the other side of an = sign on a Timucua clan drawing? (Hint: See rule C.) _____ So, would any of these people be in your clan? _____

(11) You decided grandmother #2 is in your clan. Let's keep investigating. From grandmother #2, go down, across, down. Try to figure out which people are connected by those lines. Look at this list of names: mom, uncle #4, aunt #4, aunt #5, uncle #5. Decide which ones would be in your clan and circle those names on the list. Then color them green in figure I. Remember, never cross to the other side of an = sign.

(12) You went down, across, down to get to uncle #4. Why wouldn't aunt #4 be in your clan? (Hint: See rule C.)

_____

_____

Since aunt #4 wouldn't be in your clan, would her daughter,

cousin #4, be in your clan? (Hint: See rule A.) _____
Why not?_____

_____

(13) You went down, across, down to get to aunt #5. Why
wouldn't uncle #5 be in your clan? (Hint: See rule C.)

_____

_____

Since aunt #5 would be in your clan, would her kids, cousin #5a
and cousin #5b, be in your clan? (Hint: Their mother would be.)
_____ If yes, color them green.

(14) You went down, across, down to get to your mom. Would she
be in your clan? _____ You would have to cross an = sign
to get to your dad. Would he be in your clan?_____
Why not?_____

_____

(15) Start at your mom. Go down, across, down. Color a green
outline around the square marked "you." Look at this list of
names and decide which people would be in your clan: sister-in-
law #6, brother #6, brother #7, sister #8, brother-in-law #8.
Then circle their names, and color them green in figure I.
Remember, never cross to the other side of an = sign.

(16) If you said brothers and sisters would be in your clan, but
brothers-in-law and sisters-in-law wouldn't be, you chose the
correct answer. Now it gets tricky: What about nieces and

nephews? Would they be in your clan? Remember rule A, kids are always in their mother's clan. In question 15, you found that your sister (#8) would be in your clan. Would her kids, nephew #8 and niece #8, be in your clan too? (Hint: Their mother would be.)
_____ If yes, color them green.

(17) Your brother #6 also has kids, niece #6 and nephew #6. Would they be in your clan? (Hint: Their mother wouldn't be.)

_____

(18) Look at figure I. The colored circles, triangles, and squares would all be in your Timucua clan, the Earth Clan. Circle the names of the people in this list who would be in your clan: great-grandfather, great-grandmother, grandfather #1, grandmother #1, grandfather #2, grandmother #2, great-uncle, uncle #3, aunt #3, dad, mom, uncle #4, aunt #4, aunt #5, uncle #5, sister-in-law #6, brother #6, brother #7, sister #8, brother-in-law #8, you, cousin #4, cousin #5a, cousin #5b, niece #6, nephew #6, nephew #8, niece #8.

Go ahead and check your answers on page 120. If you were a little confused, don't be surprised. This is the hardest Detective Directive in the book. You can try it again on the figure that follows if you would like to. Sometimes it helps to try the hard stuff again.

Figure I. Timucua clans

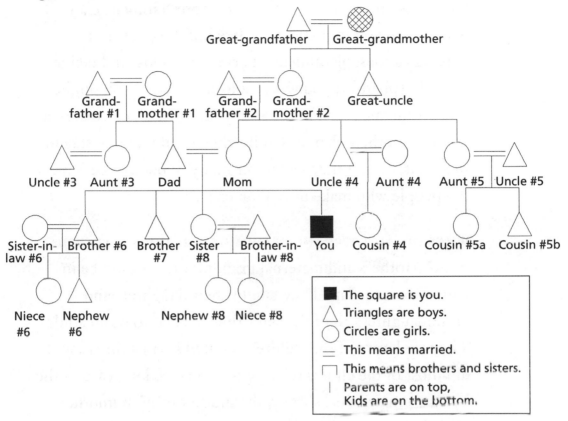

Detective, pat yourself on the back. If you've made it this far, you're sure to complete your mission!

Figuring out who would be in your clan may seem complicated to you, but it was easy for the Timucua. Just as you know who your aunt is and who your grandfather is, the Timucua kids knew who was in their clan.

WHAT JOBS DID TIMUCUA CLANS DO? Your Timucua clan would help you to do big jobs, like building new huts, making canoes, planting and harvesting fields, and taking care of orphans. If you visited another village, you might meet someone there who was in your clan. Since you are a member of their clan, or family, they would let you stay in their hut, even if they had never met you before. Let's meet the people who make up a Timucua clan.

WHAT DID MOTHERS AND GRANDMOTHERS DO IN A TIMUCUA CLAN? Mothers and maternal grandmothers would be in your Timucua clan. They taught their daughters and granddaughters all of the skills they needed to be an adult. They took care of the children, hunted small animals, and did most of the chores relating to food or taking care of the hut. In a matrilineal society, the mother or grandmother probably also owned the family hut and worked with other women to make big decisions like when to plant the fields, when to travel, who could marry whom, how to settle grown-up arguments, and many other things.

WHAT DID FATHERS AND GRANDFATHERS DO IN A TIMUCUA CLAN? We know that fathers and paternal grandfathers would not be in your Timucua clan. Instead of being in charge of teaching you and deciding punishments, the dads and grandfathers were more like your friends. You might go fishing with them and tell them your secrets.

WHAT DID UNCLES DO IN A TIMUCUA CLAN? Your mother's brother is your uncle in a Timucua clan. If you are a boy, your uncle would teach you all of the skills you'd need to be an adult. If you got into trouble, he would decide the punishment and help you learn right from wrong.

Fathers, grandfathers, and uncles made most of the decisions about war and hunting. They provided meat for their people and kept the village safe. They also made tools and weapons.

HOW DID TIMUCUA PEOPLE GET MARRIED? Remember, you could not marry anyone in your own Timucua clan. Timucua people probably got married when they were about fifteen years old. A young man would build a hut for the girl he wanted to marry. All of the people in his clan would help. After the two young people got married, the hut belonged to the wife. For the wedding ceremony, the man would hunt a deer for her, and she would make him a meal from corn. This was how they promised to take care of each other.

WHAT WERE THE HUSBAND'S JOBS? The husband would hunt large animals, bringing meat for food, animal skins for clothing and blankets, and animal bones for needles and tools. He made weapons for hunting and for fighting. He would protect the village from enemies and dangerous animals so his wife and their children would be safe.

WHAT WERE THE WIFE'S JOBS? The wife would collect fruits, nuts, and vegetables, grind corn, dry and cook meats, weave baskets, make pottery and tools, cure animal skins into leather, sew clothes, make plant medicines, bring water to the hut, and take care of their children.

Detective Directive 18: Does it sound like the men and women did equal work? _____ Look over this chapter again. On the lines below, write the activities done by men, by women, and by the whole clan.

Men	Women	Clan

Look at the table you just made. Who do you think had more work to do, the men or the women?

_____

If you said "the women," you're right. The women had more things to do, but they were safer things. Women's jobs kept them near the village so they could take care of the children and be safe. Men had less work, but their jobs were more dangerous, like hunting and fighting battles. It was a kind of trade. The men had less work, but the women were safer.

The Timucua split up jobs to make sure the children were safe. Today, since kids go to safe schools during the day, men and women can do any job they want.

5

Children

What Were Timucua Kids Like?

WHAT KIND OF CHORES DID THE KIDS DO? Timucua kids were a lot like kids today. They played games, got into arguments, did chores, and learned to be grown-ups.

They had to grow up much faster than kids today. By the time they were eleven or twelve, they were already doing grown-up work, like hunting, making pottery, planting and **harvesting** crops, and helping to make canoes and huts. By the time they were fifteen or sixteen, they were expected to act like grown-ups all the time.

 Detective Directive 19: Look at this list of what Timucua kids and modern kids do during the day.

Timucua kids	Modern kids
(1) Get up before the sun.	(1) Get up after the sun comes up.
(2) Sweat outside in the sun, picking berries or corn, carrying trash to the midden (trash pile), grinding corn, scraping hides, carrying water, making rope, and so on.	(2) Sit in an air-conditioned class and learn to read, write, and do math.
(3) Eat deer meat, grits, and grapes.	(3) Eat pizza, steak, oranges, and ice cream.
(4) Practice weaving, pottery-making, or making chert arrow points.	(4) Do homework.
(5) Listen to stories told by elders.	(5) Watch television.
(6) Sleep on a bench in a hut with no air conditioning, no toilet, no bug spray, and no electricity.	(6) Sleep on a soft bed in a cool house with lights, toilets, and no bugs.

*Who has it easier, Timucua kids or kids today?*_____

_____

WHAT KINDS OF GAMES DID TIMUCUA KIDS PLAY? They played games that taught them the skills they needed to be grown-ups.

We don't know much about the games the girls played. They probably played with dolls like kids do today. This could teach them to be good mothers. "Playing house" could teach them to run a home, feed, clothe, and take care of a family. They might have played the "Quiet Game," like other southeastern Native American groups did. This taught them to sneak up quietly on a duck or rabbit they wanted to hunt. The girls must have played many other games, but the French didn't write them down.

We know a little more about the games the boys played, because the French drew a picture and wrote some stories about them.

Detective Directive 20: Look at the French picture in figure 7. Can you think of three games the boys might be playing? Write them down.

_____

_____

_____

If you said a ball game, arrow practice, races, or canoeing, you were really investigating well. The "Ball Game" was played by throwing a ball at a high target. The ball was about the size of a baseball and was probably made of clay and leather. The target was a flat piece of wood or matting at the top of a post.

Detective Directive 21: Pretend you are throwing a baseball overhand. Move your arm in the throwing motion. Now pretend you are throwing a spear. Did you move your arm the same way

Figure J. French drawing showing games the Timucua boys played

in both throws? ____ __ How could the ball game help Timucua
boys learn to hunt? (Hint: Look ahead at figure V on page 95 to
see a spear.) _____

_____

_____

The boys also practiced shooting arrows at targets to get
better at hunting. They had races to see who was the fastest.
Today people run for exercise or just for fun. When the
Timucua kids ran, they probably had fun, too. But they
were learning to run fast so they could chase down a deer
they had wounded or get away from an enemy who was
chasing them.

Detective Directive 22: Timucua kids also practiced to see who could hold their breath the longest. Can you think of a way this could help people who lived near a river?

_____

_____

Detective Directive 23: The Timucua kids probably had great games of hide-and-seek in the forest. How could these games help them learn to hunt and track animals?

_____

_____

Detective Directive 24: Look at this list of activities. Circle the ones that both Timucua kids and kids today could do.

(1) Arm wrestle

(2) Play ball

(3) Build sand castles

(4) Canoe

(5) Climb trees

(6) Dance

(7) Play tag

(8) Go on dates

(9) Go to the movies

(10) Do gymnastics

(11) Play hide and seek

(12) Play leap frog

(13) Listen to music

(14) Build forts

(15) Play computer games

(16) Play Nintendo

(17) Play with dolls

(18) Have foot races

(19) Read books

(20) Ride bikes

(21) Ride horses

(22) Have splash fights

(23) Have swim races

(24) Watch television

Timucua children were much like children today. They got into arguments and did chores. They played games and studied. They wanted to look cool and sometimes got into trouble. They worked hard and even had boyfriends or girlfriends. Kids are kids, no matter when they live.

6

Villages and Homes

Where Did the Timucua Live?

The people who spoke the Timucua language lived in northern Florida and southern Georgia. They almost always lived near the water: along rivers, near marshes, or next to the ocean. They may have lived in large villages with 50 to 250 people or in small groups with only a few families. Some archaeologists think they lived in small groups part of the year and in big villages during the rest.

WHAT WERE THEIR HOMES LIKE? Their houses were circular, not rectangular like homes today. Most had only one room. To make the walls, Timucua pounded tree trunks upright into the ground and tied them together at the top. Then they wove grapevines and thin trees around the poles. (See figure K.) While the hut was being built, the walls looked like a fishing net, with open squares made by crisscrossing branches. Then the Timucua took palm fronds and wove the stems over and under the vines. The palms were woven in so tightly that after the roof was **thatched,** it kept all the rain out. There was a low opening left for a door and one in the ceiling to let the smoke out. These huts didn't have windows. The Timucua might have used mud or clay to seal small leaks in the palm thatching, but archaeologists have not found any clues to prove this.

> **Thatched means "woven with palm leaves."**

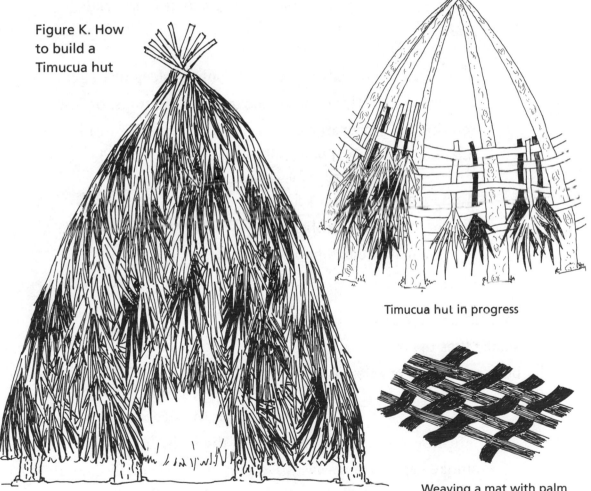

Figure K. How to build a Timucua hut

Timucua hut in progress

Palm fronds were woven over and under to thatch a roof.

Weaving a mat with palm fronds (leaves)

Detective Directive 25: Look at figure K. How many rooms does this hut have? _____ Six to eight people probably lived in this one-room hut. It was 19 to 25 feet wide. Have your parents help you measure your bedroom. How many feet across is it? _____ How many people live in your room? _____ Who has more space in their homes, Timucua people or modern Floridians? _____ If six to eight people lived in your room, it would be very crowded. Would you want to spend much time inside? _____ Or would you rather be outside in the fresh air? _____

The Timucua usually came inside only to sleep or to get out of the rain. If they were playing, making tools, or just relaxing, they probably did it outside their hut or inside the big council house. They could cook inside or outside.

Along the inner wall of their huts, they had sleeping benches that were probably made out of rivercane. Rivercane is like bamboo. This plant is tall, thin, and smooth, with no branches to poke you in the back. The Timucua probably covered these cane beds with deer or bear fur to make them comfortable. A **smudge fire** was often lit under the sleeping benches.

> **Smudge fires are tiny, smoky fires that keep bugs away from people.**

This tiny corncob fire didn't burn the beds. Instead, its smoke kept the bugs away. Do you think it kept all the bugs away? _____ Probably not, but it helped a lot. There weren't any closets in the hut, but food, tools, weapons, and toys could be stored under the benches or hung on the walls.

Small storage houses, called "*pahas*," were probably built near the hut to hold corn, dried meat, and other foods for winter. Sometimes the storage containers or houses were sealed shut with dried mud, so that even the tiniest bug could not get in and spoil the stored food. Today we can buy fresh food year-round, so we don't have to worry about trying to make food last for six or seven months. It took a lot of work to dry food out so that it would last. If you didn't prepare your food well, it would rot. Then what would you eat in the middle of winter? There weren't any grocery stores back then. Sometimes these storage *pahas* were hidden deep in the forest or on small islands. The chief also kept a special storehouse of grain every year to provide food for anyone who ran out.

Detective Directive 26: Look at figure L. In this French picture, the huts in the village were built fairly close together (about 70 feet apart). All of the trees and shrubs around the huts were cut down. The Timucua shared their environment with snakes, bears, and panthers. Can you think of a reason why they would clear the trees away from their huts?

_____

_____

_____

Figure L. French drawing showing a Timucua village

This French picture may have some mistakes. The artist, DeBry, may have added the fence and made the council house square. Real Timucua villages probably had no fences, and the council house was always round.

☞ Cool Fact: The reason we have yards around houses today is because the Native Americans taught newcomers to clear a space around their homes. That way, you can see anything trying to sneak up on you.

The chief had a larger hut than everyone else. It may have had four rooms instead of just one, but it was still a round, palm-thatched building like the others. Sometimes the Timucua would dig down into the ground before they built a chief's house. If the floor was below ground level, the chief's house would stay cool even on hot days. This digging was a lot of work, so only the chief got to have a cool floor.

WHAT IS A COUNCIL HOUSE? Many large villages had a council house in the middle of all the small family huts. It was big enough for all the people in the village to fit inside. There were rows of benches along the inside of this giant round hut. People could sit inside for meetings, feasts, and dances. Visitors could sleep there, too. The Spanish said that some council houses were big enough to seat 2,000 people!

WERE THERE OTHER KINDS OF VILLAGES IN FLORIDA? The Englishman John Sparks said that instead of living in lots of small family huts, many families lived together in a few really big huts that could hold over 100 people. This way of living might have helped by using less firewood, because you can cook together and heat only one house. Maybe the larger building was stronger in a hurricane. Figuring out why Florida Native Americans might have used big houses is a good task for future historical detectives.

WERE THERE EVEN MORE KINDS OF VILLAGES? Some archaeologists think so. They say that the Timucua may not have lived near the council house. Instead, groups of families might have lived near the fields they planted. They came to the council house for feasts and meetings, but they didn't live right near it. In this type of village, the council house would be like the capitol of a spread-out town.

Just like today's Floridians, the Timucua had many different kinds of towns and buildings. You probably could find all of these buildings in or near a large Timucua village: regular round houses, bigger chiefs' houses, giant council houses, storage buildings, guard huts to keep the fields safe, special huts for women, a charnel house (see chapter 14), huts for smoking meat, and maybe sweat lodges. There probably would be small gardens near the huts for the special plants each family wanted. There also would be an open field for playing ball and huge gardens for the whole village.

HOW DO WE KNOW ABOUT THE DIFFERENT KINDS OF TIMUCUA HUTS? Archaeologists have found marks in the ground where the huts' big poles used to be. (Look at the big posts supporting the hut in figure K.) These scientists can measure between the post marks to see how big each hut was. They even can find out how many huts were in a village by counting the marks. We also know about these huts because the French wrote stories and drew pictures of them.

Detective Directive 27: Look at the French picture in figure L. What do you see around the village? _____ This fence is called a "palisade," and it looks like it is made out of giant posts. In northeast Florida, archaeologists never have found any sign of a palisade. They can find the small post marks from the

huts, but they can't find any big post marks from the palisade fence. Do you think the French artist, DeBry, may have made a mistake when he drew the palisade? _____ If you said "yes," then you agree with many archaeologists who study the Timucua today. DeBry **engraved** *pictures of many different Native American cultures. He might have borrowed the palisade idea from some other native group. We can't be sure, but today we think the Timucua did not make palisade fences.*

Detective Directive 28: Look at figure L again. What shape is the council house in the picture? _____
Archaeologists have never found post marks from a rectangular hut. They have found the post marks from a giant circular hut. Do you think the French artist made a mistake when he drew the rectangular council house? _____ If you said "yes," then you agree with most archaeologists who study Florida's Native Americans.

WHAT WAS LIFE LIKE IN A TIMUCUA VILLAGE? Some French and Spanish wrote that the Timucua lived in their villages for only part of the year and disappeared into the woods for the rest. No one is really sure if this is true. Some Timucua families might have gone to visit relatives, hunt deer, fish for oysters, or go to battle during parts of the year. It's hard to imagine everyone in the village leaving. Who would protect the huts and gardens?

Detective Directive 29: Imagine being a Timucua kid. If you had to leave your home for three months each year and live someplace else, what would you take with you? Don't take too much, because you have to carry it! _____

_____

_____

_____

We don't know for sure whether everyone left the village. We do believe that small groups (a few families) left the villages for a while to visit good fishing spots. But did everyone leave the village for months? Maybe some did and some didn't. That's a good question for future historical detectives.

7

Foods

What Did the Timucua Eat?

WHERE DID THE TIMUCUA GROW PLANTS? They usually planted crops in fields near their villages. The villages on the east side of the St. Johns River had sandy soil, which is not good for growing crops. (Go back to figure C on page 14 to see where the St. Johns River is.) Because of this, they had smaller gardens and depended more on gathering wild plants. The villages west of the river had rich soil, so it was easy for the western Timucua to be excellent farmers.

WHAT KINDS OF PLANTS DID THEY GROW? The Timucua grew corn, beans, squash, pumpkins, and sunflowers. In the spring, they planted seeds in small hills of dirt. The little hills kept the seeds from washing away in the rain. Then the corn grew up straight and tall, and bean vines crawled right up the cornstalks to reach the sun. About halfway through the summer, the corn would be ripe. The Timucua called

The Timucua could plant two crops of corn, one in early summer and one in late summer. Florida's weather is very warm, so the growing season lasts a long time.

this early **corn.** After they picked it (and the beans growing nearby), they planted a new crop of corn and beans. This crop, called late **corn,** would not be ripe until the autumn. By then, all of the crops were ready to harvest. So, they picked the squash, pumpkins, sunflowers, beans, and late corn at the same time. After the harvest, they probably had a huge feast.

 Detective Directive 30: The Timucua burned the fields each spring before they planted a new crop. Can you think of two reasons for them to do this?

_____

_____

(Hint: What about weeds? What about fertilizer?)

WHAT PLANTS DID THE TIMUCUA GATHER FROM THE WOODS? The Timucua searched for many plants in the forest and along the edges of rivers and streams. They used these plants to make jellies, vegetables, tea, gum, grains, seasonings, sweets, and medicines.

Look at the lists below. The <u>underlined</u> plants could be found only in the <u>summer</u> or <u>fall</u>; they weren't ripe for eating during other parts of the year.

For fresh fruit and jellies, they gathered <u>grapes</u>, <u>blueberries</u>, blackberries, <u>plums</u>, <u>persimmons</u>, and many more fruits.

☞ Cool Fact: Did you notice that apples, bananas, and oranges are not on this list? The weather is too cold for bananas and too hot for apples, and oranges didn't grow here then either. The Spanish brought oranges to Florida.

For cooked vegetables and fungus, they gathered <u>wild onions</u>, cabbage palm heart, dandelion leaves, mushrooms, prickly pear, and more.

For teas, they gathered pine needles, <u>goldenrod flowers</u>, <u>winged sumac's lemony fruits</u>, <u>horsemint</u>, yaupon holly leaves (for the black drink), and more.

For gum, they gathered sweetgum sap, <u>"bear claw flower" sap</u>, and other types of sap.

For nuts, grains, and flour (to make bread), they gathered <u>acorns</u>, <u>hickory nuts</u>, <u>cattail roots and flowers</u>, <u>chinquapin nuts</u>, <u>pigweed</u>, <u>wild rice</u>, and more.

For seasonings, they gathered bay leaves, wild garlic, <u>peppergrass seeds</u>, saltwort, wax myrtle, and other herbs.

For sweets, they gathered maple tree sap, hickory tree sap, **honey,** and other things.

> Honeybees were brought to this country from Europe. They didn't start out here.

☞ Cool Fact: They could make sugar and syrup from the sap of a maple tree. We have red maples in North Florida. A different kind of maple, called a "sugar maple," grows farther north. Sugar maples make sweeter syrup than red maples do.

 Detective Directive 31: The Timucua couldn't go to a grocery store to get food. They had to find plants growing wild in the forest. If the plant was not ripe, they couldn't have any. If you were a Timucua, and you wanted some gum in the middle of winter, what kind of tree would you get sap from?

_____ If you wanted a cooked vegetable in wintertime, choose one that you could find.

_____ If you wanted to put seasonings on that vegetable, what seasoning plants could you use?

_____ We are lucky today. If it is not apple season in the United States, it is apple season somewhere else— maybe South America or Australia. So today, we can always get apples if we really want them.

IMPORTANT: NEVER EAT A WILD PLANT. IT COULD BE POISONOUS!

WHAT WATER ANIMALS DID THE TIMUCUA EAT? They ate alligators, clams, crabs, crayfish, dolphins, ducks and their eggs, fish, frogs, mussels, oysters, seals, sharks, shrimp, turtles and their eggs, beached pilot whales, and whelks.

WHAT LAND ANIMALS DID THEY EAT? They ate bears, deer, opossums, quail, rabbit, raccoon, snakes, squirrels, tortoises and their eggs, turkeys, and wild pigs.

☞ Cool Fact 1: The Spanish brought wild pigs to Florida; pigs (boars) didn't used to live here.
Cool Fact 2: Armadillos did not live in Florida then either. A circus brought them from Mexico in the early 1900s, and they escaped. Now they're everywhere!
Cool Fact 3: Bison (buffalo) are not on this list because there were very few bison in northeastern Florida and southeastern Georgia. They need large grassy fields to graze, and Florida is too swampy. Swamps are not a good habitat for bison. If the Timucua had traveled to the Tallahassee area (in northwestern Florida), where the Apalachee Indians lived, they might have found a few bison there to hunt.

Detective Directive 32: Pretend you are a Timucua. It's a breezy fall day, and there will be a big feast to celebrate your chief's wedding. You need to come up with a menu for the feast. You should have at least one crop that the Timucua grew, one wild fruit, one wild vegetable, one bread (like acorn bread), one tea, one water animal, and one land animal. Be sure to use seasonings on your meat so it will taste good for the chief and the guests.

The tea will be

_____

_____

The crop will be

_____

_____

_____

The wild fruit will be

_____

_____

The wild vegetable will be

_____

_____

The bread will be

_____

_____

The water animal with seasonings will be

_____

_____

The land animal with a different seasoning will be

_____

_____

Well, now you have a menu, but you still haven't cooked the food. Here's how the Timucua cooked:

Teas were made by boiling fresh or dried plants.

Vegetables were boiled, because wild plants are often tough, bitter, or poisonous until you cook them for a while.

Nuts and grains were pounded into flour and cooked well to remove bitterness. Bread dough could be baked into a loaf, fried in bear fat to make fritters, or boiled to make dumplings.

Fruits were eaten fresh, made into jelly, or dried in the sun so they would not rot. Grapes dried into raisins; plums dried into prunes. Some vegetables, like corn and squash, were also dried and lasted all through the winter without refrigeration.

Corn could be eaten raw or cooked. It was often allowed to dry until it was hard. Then it was pounded into grits or corn flour. Corn flour makes cornbread.

Some seeds were eaten. These included the seeds from corn (kernels), beans, squash, pumpkins, and sunflowers. Some seeds were saved to be planted next year.

Meats and Fish could be roasted over a fire or cooked in a stew. To preserve meat for the winter, the Timucua would cut it into strips and dry it over a smoky fire. Meat preserved this way is called "jerky." Have you ever tasted beef jerky? That's dried meat. (See figure M.) You can cook fish or meat in a stew by cutting it up in a pot of water. Then you add vegetables, spices, and corn and boil the water until the meat is cooked. Some shellfish, like

Figure M. French drawing showing how the Timucua preserved meat

oysters and whelks, could be eaten raw, steamed over a
fire, or cooked into a stew.

 *Detective Directive 33: Go back to Detective Directive 32. On
the line underneath each of your menu choices, write how you
would prepare the plant or meat. Did you eat it fresh, boil it, dry
it, or roast it over a fire? (Hint: See above for ideas.)*

 *Detective Directive 34: Look at figure M again. We said before
that the Timucua usually cut animal meat into thin strips before
drying it over a fire. The artist probably left the animals whole in
the picture so that we could guess at what animals the Timucua*

were eating. Can you tell which five animals are shown in this picture? _____

_____

_____

Did you say "dog" as one of your answers? It may have been a fox instead. In southern Georgia, archaeologists found a grave where a dog was buried. The dog had been shot with a Spanish gun. If the Timucua cared enough about their dogs to bury them, do you think they normally would eat them? _____

_____

WHEN DID THE TIMUCUA EAT? The Spanish and French wrote that the Timucua men only ate one meal each day, usually at night. Women and children probably ate more often. Meals weren't sit-down dinners. People just ate when they were hungry. If it was a big feast, everyone ate at the same time. Sometimes many families would cook together, sharing their food. They might do this if they were cooking for a big feast or if food was running out.

> **Carbohydrates are foods like bread, rice, nuts, and corn.**

Detective Directive 35: Food sharing is important when food is running out. The chief usually kept a storehouse of corn to share with people who didn't have enough. That helped, but it wasn't always enough. The most nutritious Timucua meals had three parts: meat or fish, vegetables or fruits, and **carbohydrates.** *In the activity that follows, none of the families will get nutritious* meals if they eat alone. What kind of meal will they have if they share? Figure out what category of food each family has. Then write it under the correct heading: meats and fish, fruits and vegetables, or carbohydrates.

Family 1 has palm cabbage.   Family 5 has grits.

Family 2 has dried fish.   Family 6 has blueberry jelly.

Family 3 has peppergrass.   Family 7 has dried deer meat.

Family 4 has acorn bread.   Family 8 has wild rice.

If they share, they will all get:

Meats and fish	Fruits and vegetables	Carbohydrates
_____	_____	_____
_____	_____	_____
_____	_____	_____
_____	_____	_____
_____	_____	_____

The next time you sit down to dinner, try to figure if you have a meat or fish, a fruit or vegetable, and a carbohydrate. Different people like different kinds of foods. What is your favorite food? _____ Is this a food that the Timucua kids could have gotten? _____ (Hint: They didn't have chocolate.)

8

Medicines and Ceremonial Teas

How Did the Timucua Make Aspirin?

HOW DID THE TIMUCUA GET MEDICINES? Medicines were made from many different plants. Most Timucua knew something about medicine plants, just like you know what cough medicine is. Timucua women knew more about plants than the men did, because women worked with plants when they collected food. Since they understood many things about plants, women made many of the medicines.

WHAT IS A SHAMAN? If someone was very sick, injured in battle, or having a baby, the shaman would be in charge. He studied the plants to make medicines, but he also prayed for the person to get better. You could ask the shaman to bring you luck, put a curse on someone, or make someone fall in love. You had to pay him, just like we pay doctors today, but the Timucua did not have money. You could pay him with a woven basket or a cooked turkey.

HOW DID THE TIMUCUA MAKE MEDICINES? Medicines were made in many ways. Some plants were burned (like **tobacco**), and the patient breathed in the steam. Some plants were mashed into a paste and put directly on a

> Today we know that tobacco can cause cancer. The Timucua did not know this.

wound, the way you put medicine on a cut. This is called a **poultice** (POLE-tis). Other plants were boiled into a tea you could drink. For example, willow bark tea has aspirin in it.

Medicines could be made from the flowers, leaves, roots, stems, or bark of special plants. The Timucua studied plants all of their lives. Today most people don't know much about wild plants, so it is not safe to make your own food and medicine from the forest.

NEVER EAT A WILD PLANT. IT COULD BE POISONOUS!

Here are a few medicine plants used by Florida's Native Americans. Look next to each plant name to find out what problem each one cured:

Buttonbush (toothache)   Ground-cherry leaves (burns)

Corydalis (stomachache)   Willow tree bark (headache)

Goldenrod (coughing)   Witch hazel (itching)

Detective Directive 36: Look at the list above. If you burned yourself, what plant would you need to make a cool wash to clean the burn? _____ If you had a toothache, what plant would you need to make a medicine tea?

_____

WHAT WAS THE BLACK DRINK? This ceremonial tea, called "cassina" (ka-SEE-na) was made from the leaves of yaupon holly. This holly has a chemical in its leaves called **caffeine.** Today caffeine is in many canned drinks and teas. It is also in chocolate bars and coffee. The Timucua and many other southeastern Native American groups made a special caffeine drink from the leaves. They roasted the leaves to make the caffeine blend better into hot water.

> Today people roast coffee beans for the same reason—to make the caffeine dissolve better in water. This gives the coffee more caffeine.

Timucua men sipped the "black drink" at meetings, and it gave them a little caffeine. Caffeine makes you sweat. The Timucua believed that they were sweating out all of the dirt in their skin AND getting rid of all of their fear and laziness. So this drink purified them and made them feel clean.

The Timucua used this drink in another way, too. Sometimes, before a big battle or a hunt, the men would drink several cups of the black drink, really hot, really fast. Drinking anything that quickly can make you feel sick. The

scientific name for the black drink plant is *Ilex vomitoria*.
What do you think the black drink could make the
Timucua men do? _____
Right—it could make them **vomit**, or throw up. They
tried not to throw up, because if they did everyone would
think that they were weak.

The reason they drank so much was to get the caffeine.
After drinking lots of the black drink, they would have
enough energy to run all day without eating. Since
they didn't have horses or cars, the black drink was
their way of being able to travel fast. Figure N shows the

Figure N. French drawing showing the black drink ceremony

black drink ceremony. Can you find the two Timucua men who are throwing up? _____ Is throwing up fun? _____ Definitely not! But the Timucua had to find ways to survive. They didn't have mechanical (machine) technology, like we do today. Instead, they had botanical (plant) technology. They used plant science to survive.

9

Hunting

How Did the Timucua Catch Animals for Food?

HOW DID THE TIMUCUA HUNT LAND ANIMALS? They hunted large land animals with spears, spear-throwers, clubs, and bows and arrows. If they were hunting for a deer, they would look in a deer's favorite spots. Since deer love to eat acorns, would an oak forest be a good place to hunt them? _____ (Hint: Acorns come from oak trees.)

How did the Timucua hunt deer? Sometimes, they would sneak up on a deer by wearing a deer cloak. This was the whole fur of a deer, with the legs and head attached. (See figure O.) The Timucua men crept along, letting the deer's legs hang down like normal. They pretended to be a deer, so they could sneak up on their prey. When they got close enough to the deer, they would try to kill it with their bows and arrows.

Figure O. French drawing showing a Timucua deer hunt

The Timucua also hunted smaller forest animals, like squirrels, raccoons, opossums, and turkeys. They sometimes used snares and traps so they didn't have to be nearby when the animal was caught.

Sometimes the Timucua would set a part of the forest on fire. This is called a "fire drive." The deer, turkeys, rabbits, pigs, and raccoons would run away from the fire. The Timucua men would be waiting for them. When the animals ran by, the Timucua would have a good shot at them. After the fire had burned the forest, lots of grasses and small plants would grow. Deer, mice, rabbits, and tortoises like to eat these plants. So if the Timucua kept an area burned off, some animals would come there to eat all year. The Timucua didn't put up fences around the animals, but they did change the habitat so animals would want to stay close by.

IMPORTANT: YOU SHOULD NEVER START A FOREST FIRE ON PURPOSE TODAY!

HOW DID THE TIMUCUA HUNT WATER ANIMALS? **Oysters** grow in salt marshes in big clumps with their shells stuck together. The Timucua probably used a whelk shell hammer to crack off big chunks of oysters and bring them home. Fish were hunted with spears, nets, traps, and hooks and lines. They didn't have fishing poles. The men did the really dangerous hunting for deer, alligators, and sharks. But the women and boys probably helped to catch smaller animals with traps, hooks, and lines, and maybe even with spears and slings. (A sling is a leather strap that is used to hurl a stone.)

> The oyster shells they cracked open make up the big shell middens, or trash piles, that archaeologists study today.

Timucua men hunted alligators very carefully! Alligators have tough scales on their backs. These scales protect them from spears and arrows, but an alligator's belly is softer. The trick is to get an alligator to roll over for you! First, a brave Timucua man had to get really close to the alligator—to act as bait. When the alligator opened its mouth to try to eat the bait, the other men would shove one end of a long tree trunk in its mouth. Thinking the tree was food, the gator would bite down really hard. The pole would get stuck in its mouth and throat. Then the alligator couldn't bite anyone. The Timucua hunters still had to be very careful of the alligator's powerful tail. They grabbed the tree trunk and turned it over, and that turned the alligator over, too. Once it was turned over, the hunters could spear its soft belly. (See figure P.)

Figure P. French drawing showing how the Timucua hunted alligators

IMPORTANT: IT IS AGAINST THE LAW TO HUNT OR TEASE AN ALLIGATOR TODAY.

Detective Directive 37: Look at the alligator hunt in figure P. See if you can answer the questions below about the facts and mistakes in this picture.

(1) What three weapons did the Timucua use to hunt the alligator once it was flipped over? _____

_____

_____

(2) Did women help with the alligator hunt?_____

_____

(3) In the alligator hunt picture, the alligator has eyebrows, ears, and long fingers. Do you think alligators looked like this 400 years ago? _____ Definitely not! The man who engraved this picture had never seen a real alligator, so he just did the best he could. The alligator in the front would also be 80 feet long in real life. Today, alligators are usually 6–12 feet long. Do you think alligators were 80 feet long back then? _____ They may have been 20–30 feet long, but not 80! This was probably a drawing mistake.

(4) Are the men wearing any clothing in this picture? _____ It doesn't look like it. What small piece of clothing did the Timucua men usually wear? _____

_____ Since they are wearing loincloths in most of the other French pictures, do you think they were probably wearing some kind of clothing when they went hunting? _____

(5) Do you think the men would try to hunt more than one of these dangerous animals at a time? _____ The picture shows two, but that is probably because the artist wanted to show the whole hunt on one page. Usually, they would only hunt one alligator at a time.

From this picture, we learned how the Timucua hunted alligators. But we have to pay close attention, so all of those drawing mistakes don't give us false clues. In chapter 12, we'll investigate why there are so many mistakes in the French pictures of the Timucua.

10

Tools

How Did the Timucua Make Knives and Fishhooks?

WHAT STONE TOOLS DID THE TIMUCUA USE? They made tools out of a stone called **chert.** Chert is a lot like flint, but it doesn't chip as well. Since chert was the only kind of stone in Florida, the Timucua had to use it. It is usually white or gray. Sometimes the Timucua would heat chert in a fire to make it stronger. Heating turns the stone pink.

The Timucua would chip away at the chert with a piece of deer antler. As more chips came off, the chert began to look like a knife or the point for an arrow. **Projectile point** is the scientific name for any stone point. These points could be used to tip arrows, spears, knives, drills, or scrapers.

> A projectile point could also be made of bone, shell, or shark's teeth.

It took years of practice and skill to get good at **knapping** stone tools. Men probably made the hunting weapons. Women probably made other tools. Chert is naturally sharp, so any piece knocked off by the antler could probably be used as a knife, no matter what it looked like. (See figure Q.)

> "Knapping" means to make stone tools. You chip pieces off of a rock until it is the right tool shape.

Figure Q. Stone tools made by Florida's Native Americans

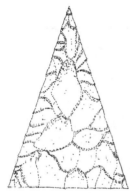

Pinellas point (made between 750 and 250 years ago)

Columbia point (made between 1,800 and 750 years ago)

Clovis point (made around 12,000 years ago)

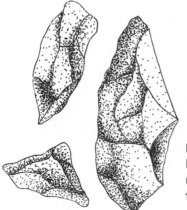

Debitage (chips left over from making a projectile point)

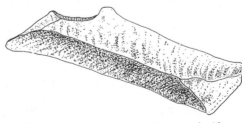

One-use knife

Detective Directive 38: Archaeologists can learn about the Timucua by looking at the trash they left behind. Reread the last three paragraphs, and try to do the detective work below.

If you found a bunch of small pink chips next to a projectile (arrow) point, what can you guess about the person making it? Was the person probably a man or a woman? _____ Was this person a small child or someone older? _____ Did this person do anything to the chert to make it stronger? What? _____ Why do you think this person was making this particular tool? _____

_____

The chips left behind after making a projectile point are called "debitage" (DEB-ee-tazh).

WHAT TOOLS WERE MADE OF BONE AND SHELL? Needles, ear pins, whistles, flutes, knives, hoes, axes, and fishhooks could be carved from animal bones. Turtle shells made great bowls and rattles. Deer antler hammers were used as tools for making projectile points. Sharp teeth and claws made knives, drills, and jewelry. Cups and bowls could be made from whelk shells. Hoes, axes, and hammers could be made by attaching a whelk shell to the end of a wooden handle. Fishing-net weights could be made from any heavy shell. Choppers, which mash and cut up vegetables and grains, could have been made from shell, chert, or wood. (See figure R.)

Figure R. Tools made from bone and shell

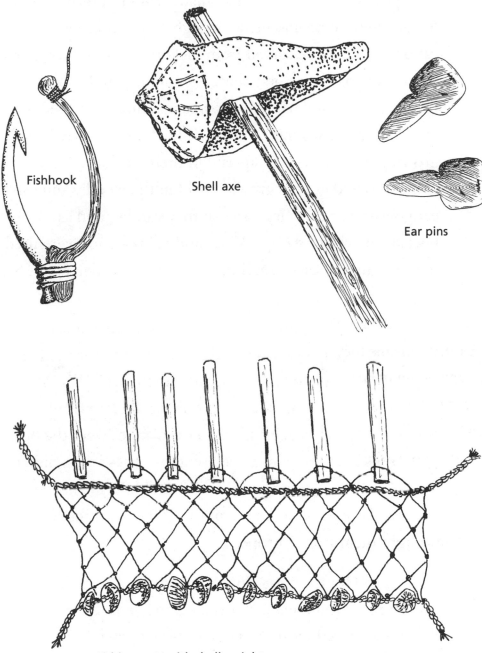

Fishhook

Shell axe

Ear pins

Fishing nets with shell weights

WHAT KIND OF TOOLS DID THEY MAKE FROM PLANTS? Arrow and spear shafts were probably made from rivercane, which looks like bamboo and grows straight and tall. Bows and canoe paddles were carved from hickory wood. **Clubs** were made from hard tree branches. Fishing nets and rope were made from twisted palm fibers. Spanish moss was used to weave cloth for women's clothes. The Timucua may have grown gourds (a type of squash) in their gardens. They could also find gourds growing wild in the woods. You can't eat gourds, but they dry hard, so they can be used as buckets, bowls, or scoops. Vines and palm fronds were used to weave mats, baskets, and the roofs of huts. (See figure S, page 85, and figure K, page 51.)

> **"Extinct" means that a type of animal or plant has died out, so there will never be any more around.**

Canoes were made from the trunks of cypress or pine trees. Canoes are called "dugouts" because the Native Americans dug out the middle of the tree trunk to make a place to sit. Canoes were the only way to travel long distances if you didn't want to walk. You couldn't ride horses, because there were no horses in the 1500s until the Spanish brought them from Europe.

☞ Cool Fact: Horses, mastodons, camels, giant armadillos, giant tortoises, and giant sloths used to live in Florida, but they became **extinct** here about 10,000 years ago. We know those animals were in Florida and Georgia because archaeologists have found their bones.

Figure 5. Timucua containers

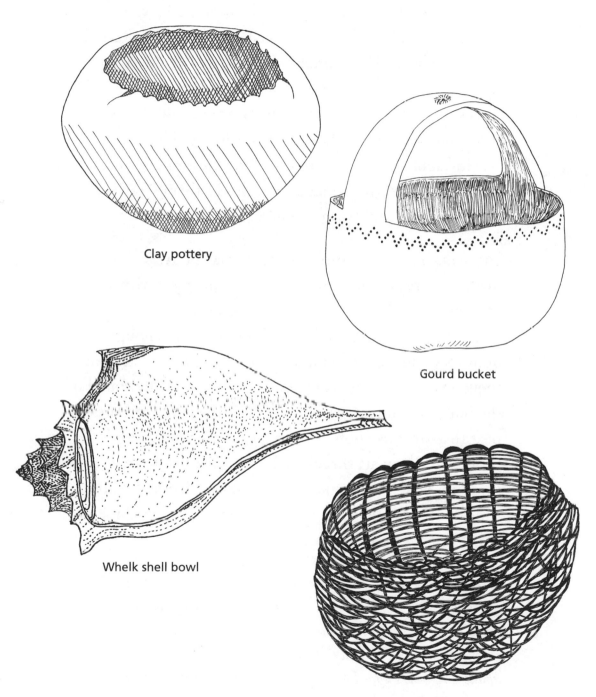

Clay pottery

Gourd bucket

Whelk shell bowl

Basket

WHAT KIND OF TOOLS DID THEY MAKE FROM ANIMAL SKIN AND GUTS? Twisted deer leather was used to make bowstrings. Bladders and stomachs made excellent water bags. Furs and skins were made into clothes, blankets, and packs. Animal tendons, or sinews, are tough and stringy and were used like a sticky rope to tie things tightly. An animal's brains were rubbed into its hide to keep it from rotting. This was called "brain-tanning," and it cured the hide into leather. Many tools and clothes were made from this leather. Scraps of hide and bone could also be boiled to make glue.

WHAT KIND OF TOOLS DID THEY MAKE FROM CLAY? They made pottery and pipes out of **clay** by mixing it with sand, shaping it, and heating it in a fire. This made the pots hard and waterproof. Pots could be very tiny or big enough to hold a stew for several families. Some pots had designs on them, and some were plain. The pots were usually round on the bottom (not flat), so they could sit down in the ashes next to a fire. Clay pots are very heavy. When these pots broke, the Timucua threw the broken pieces into their trash **midden.** When archaeologists find these pieces of Native American trash, they can tell how old the pot is by looking at the designs on it.

Detective Directive 39: Look at figure T. Each of these designs was made by Florida's Native Americans at different times. Some were made by the Timucua, and some were not. The Timucua culture started in Florida about 2,500 year ago and disappeared about 250 years ago. Let's try to investigate which pottery types were made by the Timucua and which weren't.

Figure T. Florida pottery designs

Deptford Check-Stamped (2,500 to 1,250 years ago)

Swift Creek (1,800 to 1,500 years ago)

St. Johns Plain (2,500 to 500 years ago)

Orange Period Fiber-Tempered Plain (4,000 to 2,500 years ago)

St. Johns Check-Stamped (1,250 to 500 years ago)

Start by looking at the timeline in figure U. A timeline is a tool that archaeologists use to show what things were happening at different times. This timeline goes from 4,000 years ago to today. To figure out which pottery the Timucua made, find 2,500 on the timeline and color a green dot on it. This is when the Timucua began as a culture. Now find 250 and color a green dot there. That's when the Timucua disappeared. Now connect the two dots. Your green line shows when the Timucua were in Florida: from 2,500 years ago to 250 years ago.

Arrows have been drawn to show when each pottery type was made. Any pottery arrow that is straight over your green line means that those types of pottery were made while the Timucua were here. If a pottery arrow is not over your green line, the Timucua did not make that kind of pottery.

On figure U, circle the name of each type of pottery the Timucua made. Write your answers below.
What was made by the Timucua?

_____

_____

What wasn't made by the Timucua?

_____

_____

Look at the broken pieces of pottery in figure T. Which is your favorite kind of Timucua pottery?

_____

Maybe St. Johns Plain was their favorite. They made it for a longer time than any other kind.

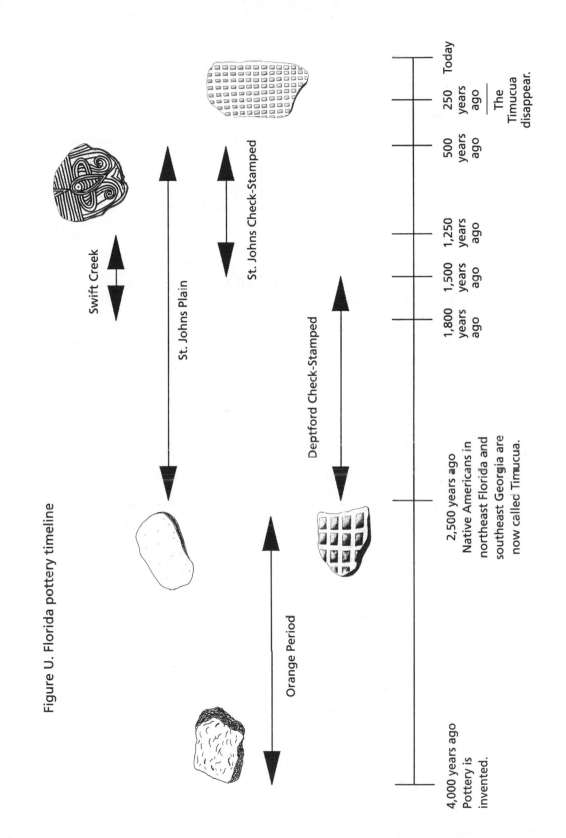

Figure U. Florida pottery timeline

Swift Creek

St. Johns Plain

St. Johns Check-Stamped

Deptford Check-Stamped

Orange Period

Today

250 years ago

The Timucua disappear.

500 years ago

1,250 years ago

1,500 years ago

1,800 years ago

2,500 years ago
Native Americans in northeast Florida and southeast Georgia are now called Timucua.

4,000 years ago
Pottery is invented.

Detective Directive 40: Let's review Timucua tools. You can look back at the beginning of this chapter for help. Write your answers on the line next to each item. What kind of tools did the Timucua make with these natural things?

(1) Antlers

_____

_____

(2) Meat

_____

_____

(3) Gourds

_____

_____

(4) Animal stomachs

_____

_____

(5) Cypress tree trunks

_____

_____

(6) Rivercane

_____

_____

(7) Shells and animal bones

_____

_____

_____

(8) Hickory wood

_____

_____

(9) Hides (furs and leather)

_____

_____

(10) Chert stone

_____

_____

(11) Clay

_____

_____

The Timucua didn't waste anything. They found a use for every little part of the animals and plants they hunted and gathered.

11

Timucua Chiefs and Beliefs

Good Luck or Good Rulers?

WHO REALLY RULED A TIMUCUA VILLAGE? Each village had a chief who was in the Deer Clan. Chiefs were usually men, but some chiefs were women. The chief had special advisors called "principal men" or "principal women." These advisors helped the chief to make big decisions. If a decision had to be made about hunting or battles, the men were in charge. On many other subjects, the women were in charge. Remember, the Timucua were matrilineal. If you're not sure what that means, check back with chapter 4. (Hint: "Matri" means "mother.")

Chiefs made **treaties** with other nearby villages. These villages worked together to protect one another and share food when one village ran out. All the villages that were friendly with each other had one **head chief**, who ruled

> **Potano was a head chief who lived northwest of Outina. Look at figure C to see where Chief Potano lived.**

them all. The head chief to the north and east of the St. Johns River was Saturiwa (Sa-chur-EE-wa). He probably had about 30 villages. The head chief to the west of the river was Outina (Oo-TEA-na). He had about 40 villages. (Look back at figure C on page 14 for a map of where the head chiefs lived.) Sometimes people in the villages paid tribute to the head chief. Tribute can be paid in things like furs, food, or shells, or it can also be respect and loyalty.

Detective Directive 41: Let's imagine we have a time machine. If we could go back in time to 1564, when the French were building Fort Caroline, what would we see? Imagine you're a French sailor. Let's go . . . .

As you and six of your fellow sailors row a small boat toward the shore, you look back at your ship. It is anchored out in the middle of the river, where the water is deep. It looks far away. You felt safe on your ship, but who knows what the Indians will do to you when you get to the land? You've heard stories, some of which are terrible. They say the Indians down south killed almost every sailor they found. Other sailors were forced to be slaves.

You row slowly. What will you find when you get there? You can see Indians standing on the marshy shore. They seem to be holding up furs and baskets of food. They are waving for you to come closer. Maybe they aren't going to hurt you after all. The Indians splash out into the muddy salt marsh water and help to pull your boat onto the land. A shy woman brings you a gourd full of water. The water is cool and sweet. You drink until you aren't thirsty anymore; then you share the water with your men.

You step out of your small boat, making sure your sword is in plain view. The Indians have weapons, but they seem more interested in trading. They lead you over to a man who is sitting beneath a palm hut. Soft animal furs cover the ground under him. He is surrounded by bowls filled with meats and fruits of every kind. A large red feather stands up from his long black hair. His skin is covered with dark dotted designs. A boy stands nearby and fans him with turkey feathers. You know this must be Chief Saturiwa. You've heard of him. The chief tells his men to set down their bows and arrows. Then he motions for you and your men to lay down your swords. What do you do?

_____

_____

_____

_____

Think of three questions you'd like to ask Chief Saturiwa. Write them here.

_____

_____

_____

_____

If your questions are not answered by the end of this book, write me a letter at this address, and I'll try to find an answer for you: Kelley G. Weitzel, University Press of Florida, 15 Northwest 15th Street, Gainesville, FL 32611-2079.

DID THE TIMUCUA FIGHT A LOT OF WARS? According to the French, they did. Saturiwa was at war with Outina. Outina was also at war with Potano (po-TAN-o). The wars the Timucua fought were not like wars today. They did not have guns or bombs. They did not try to kill everyone and take their land. Instead, they only killed a few people, to show they were stronger. Then they went home. (Figure V shows some Timucua and French weapons.)

The French didn't understand this way of fighting, and it made them angry at Chief Outina. The French had agreed to help Outina in a battle against Chief Potano. The French soldiers brought their guns, so Outina's warriors won the battle really fast. As soon as Outina had proved he could win, he was ready to go home. But the French wanted to stay and fight and steal all of Potano's food, tools, and pearls. Outina said "no" and told his warriors to go home. He had proved he was stronger than Potano, and that was all he wanted to do.

Wars may have been fought over things like these:
Which village gets to use the part of the river with the best clay?
Who gets to hunt the deer herd that crosses the river?
What if one chief steals corn from another chief's fields?
What if someone is kidnapped from another chief's village?

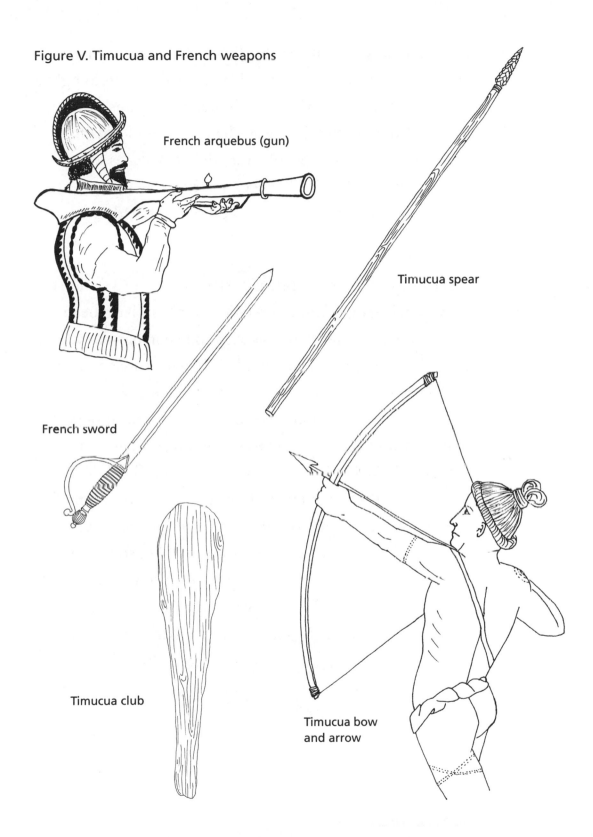

Figure V. Timucua and French weapons

French arquebus (gun)

Timucua spear

French sword

Timucua club

Timucua bow and arrow

We don't know how much the Timucua fought before the French and Spanish got to Florida. They did seem to fight a lot during the 1560s, when the French and Spanish were around. But after the Europeans had been in Florida for a while, many Timucua people were dying. Villages were getting very small. The Timucua worried less about fighting one another and more about dealing with the Spanish and the English.

WHAT KIND OF RELIGION DID THE TIMUCUA HAVE? We don't know much about Timucua religion. It might have been a nature religion. The Timucua tried to live in harmony with nature, without destroying it. The French wrote about one Timucua ceremony. The people had to hunt a large deer. Then they skinned it but left the head, legs, and antlers attached. After that they filled it with grain and sewed it shut, so that it looked like the deer was still alive. The Timucua raised the stuffed deerskin high on a post. Then the chief and the shaman began to sing songs, and the rest of the village joined in the singing. The words to these songs said the Timucua were giving a deerskin to the sun. The French soldiers thought the Timucua were worshiping the sun. Another idea is that the Timucua were thanking the sun for helping them to grow a good crop of food. (See figure W.)

Figure W. French drawing showing the Timucua
ceremony offering a deerskin to the sun

DID THE TIMUCUA BELIEVE IN MAGIC? They did believe in
signs that told whether you would have good or bad luck.
If an owl looked you in the eyes, it was a sign of very bad
luck. A popping fire could mean war was coming. If you
were in a canoe out in a storm, whistling could make the
waves calm down.

Detective Directive 42: Do the Timucua beliefs seem silly to you? Think about some **superstitions** *people have today. Can you finish each sentence below?*

If you walk under a ladder, you will have _____ luck.

If you find a four-leaf clover, you will have _____ luck.

If you open an umbrella inside, you will have _____ luck.

If a black cat crosses your path, you will have _____ luck.

If you want to keep bad luck away, you can knock on _____.

If you step on a crack, you'll break your mother's _____.

Do any of these things seem silly? Every group of people is called a "culture," and each culture has its own beliefs. If you learn about a culture, you begin to understand why it has those beliefs. For example, it is dangerous to open an umbrella inside because you might poke someone in the eye. Getting poked in the eye would be very bad luck!

12

Europeans in Florida
Why Did the Timucua Disappear?

WHAT DID COLUMBUS DO? He set sail in a Spanish ship trying to find Indonesia (the East Indies). On the way, he accidentally landed in the **West Indies**, the islands southeast of Florida. He made several trips to the West Indies and believed for his whole life that he actually had made it to Indonesia. But other people realized America was a new place. Because of Columbus's voyage, everyone in Europe found out about the New World (America). Lots of people wanted this new land for themselves.

WHAT DID THE SPANISH DO IN THE 1400S AND 1500S? After Columbus "discovered" the Americas, the Spanish wanted to claim all of the New World for themselves. They marched up into the Carolinas, across the Mississippi River, and into Mexico. They killed, kidnapped, and stole food from many of the Native American groups they found. The Spanish also forced the Mexican Indians to be their slaves and to mine silver for Spain. They sent Spanish missionaries, called "Jesuits," to teach Florida's Native Americans about Christianity. The Calusa Indians in South Florida killed some of these missionaries, so the Jesuits didn't stay in Florida very long.

WHAT DID THE FRENCH DO IN FLORIDA? In 1562, the French sailed to Florida to find a good place to build a fort. They didn't want Spain to get all the land in the New World. So they built a **monument** there to show that it was French land. (See figure E, page 22.) In 1564, they came back to build Fort Caroline. At first, Chief Saturiwa's people were helpful, sharing food and trading tools. Then the French made a treaty with Saturiwa's enemy, Chief Outina. After that, Saturiwa's people didn't trust the French any more. They had good reason not to trust them. When the French started to run out of food, they kidnapped a Timucua chief and tried to trade him for food.

The French and the Spanish didn't get along very well. Some of the French decided to attack the Spanish in St. Augustine. When they tried to sail there, a big storm crashed their ship south of the Spanish town. When the Spanish soldiers caught them, they killed almost every French person. The place where this happened is called Matanzas Inlet. In Spanish, *matanza* means "massacre," because all the French were killed.

☞ Cool Fact: You can visit St. Augustine and Matanzas Inlet today. These forts are still standing.

The few French people left at Fort Caroline were hungry and tired. They weren't strong enough to defend the fort all alone. So, when the Spanish soldiers attacked, all of the buildings inside Fort Caroline got burned down. Only a few Frenchmen escaped and sailed back to France. These men wrote stories and drew pictures that teach us a lot about the Timucua today.

☞ Cool Fact: You can visit Fort Caroline National Memorial today to see a copy of the French fort and a copy of the monument the French built in 1562.

WHO WROTE STORIES AND DREW PICTURES ABOUT THE TIMUCUA? A Frenchman named Laudonnière (Law-don-ee-ERE) kept a log, or diary, while he was in Florida. We've learned many things about the Timucua from these writings. Another Frenchman, named Jacques LeMoyne (zhak le-MO-een), drew many of the Timucua pictures you've been seeing in this book.

LeMoyne actually saw some of the things he drew. Others he made up from stories the Timucua told him. When the Spanish burned all the buildings in Fort Caroline, LeMoyne had to swim through the marsh to get to his ship in the St. Johns River.

> **The one LeMoyne picture that probably survived is the one with the French monument. Look back at figure E.**

Historians think that all but one of his drawings were burned up or lost in the marsh. Later, LeMoyne tried to remember the pictures and draw them again. He probably made some mistakes because no one can remember everything.

After LeMoyne died, a man named Theodore DeBry decided to engrave his pictures to put them in a book. DeBry wanted his book to look good, so sometimes he added trees to fill in the background if the pictures weren't finished. Since he had never been to Florida, he drew the wrong kinds of trees. He had never seen an alligator, either, so the one he drew was 80 feet long with eyebrows and ears. (See figure P, page 77.) DeBry may have made up some pictures entirely, from the stories written down by the French.

As historical detectives, we have to be really careful when we look at old drawings and read old stories. We can't just believe everything we see. It's up to us to use our "detective brains" to figure out what is true and what isn't.

 Detective Directive 43: Look at figure X. The Timucua told French soldiers that the Apalachee knew how to find gold. This picture is supposed to show the Apalachee looking for gold in a fast-moving river. Think about the rivers in Florida. Are they usually fast or slow? _____

From what you have studied so far, do you think there was any gold in Florida's rivers? _____ If you said "no," then you

Figure X. French drawing showing how the Apalachee people looked for gold

agree with most archaeologists and historians who study Florida's Native Americans. So why did the French draw this picture if it's not true? Here's an idea. The French really wanted to find gold in Florida. That was one of the main reasons they came to the New World. They kept asking the Timucua where they could find gold. What do you think the Timucua said?

_____

_____

Do you think the French believed that there was no gold? _____ Probably not. They really wanted to find gold, so they kept asking the Timucua, "Where's the gold? Where's the gold?" Do you think the Timucua got tired of hearing this after a while? _____ The Timucua may have made up stories about places where the French could find gold just to make them stop asking. They told them the Apalachee had gold in their mountains. There aren't very many mountains in Florida, even where the Apalachee lived. But the French believed what they heard because they really wanted to find gold. They named the mountains north of Florida the Appalachian Mountains. Where did they get this name? _____ Since the Apalachee lived far away, do you think any of the French people actually saw them getting gold out of a river? _____ As a historical detective, what did you learn from this picture?

(1) Do you think the Apalachee got gold from the rivers with long tubes? _____ Why or why not? _____
_____
_____

(2) Do you think the Timucua always told the truth to the French and Spanish? _____ Why or why not? _____
_____
_____

(3) Do you think that all of the French pictures are totally true? _____ Why or why not? _____
_____
_____

(4) Do you think that all of the French pictures are totally false? _____ Why or why not? _____
_____
_____

*Good historical detectives always decide for themselves. What do you think is true? Come up with good reasons and listen to other people's ideas. Do **research**, think hard, and figure it out.*

WHAT DID THE SPANISH DO AFTER THE FRENCH WERE GONE?
The Spanish sent another kind of missionary or priest, called a "Franciscan friar." These friars taught most of the Timucua and the Apalachee Indians about the Christian religion. By the 1600s these Native Americans had moved their villages to live next to a **mission** church. They grew corn for the Spanish missionaries and had to give some corn to the Spanish soldiers in St. Augustine.

They still dressed like Timucua and made their huts the same way, but slowly they were changing. They got metal tools, like hoes and knives, from the Spanish. These tools made their lives much easier and changed the way the Timucua farmed and how they did other chores. The Timucua started growing Spanish plants now, too. Some Timucua men and women went to work as servants in St. Augustine. Others worked on Spanish cattle ranches.

The Timucua still made pottery with clay, but now they made Spanish shapes—plates instead of bowls. They learned to read and write, so they could study the Bible and write letters to other Timucua. The missionaries asked them to cut their hair and pick Christian names. They told them to bury their dead in a certain way, to marry in a certain way, and to pray in a certain way. Over the years, the Timucua acted less and less like Timucua and more and more like Spanish Catholics. In fact, they even became Spanish citizens.

WHAT DID THE ENGLISH DO IN FLORIDA? The English wanted a share of the New World, too. They set up a town in the Carolinas, north of Florida and Georgia. They got the Yamassee Indians from the South Carolina area to go to Florida and kidnap Native Americans. The English sold these Native Americans as slaves. Many Timucua, Apalachee, and Guale (who-AH-lee) were captured and sold into slavery. The Native Americans who were still living in Florida were afraid of the English. They moved their homes to live near the Spanish fort, St. Augustine, because they felt safer there.

In 1763, Spain made a treaty with England and gave Florida to them. At that time, there were 89 Native Americans from many different native groups living near St. Augustine. They decided to leave Florida and go with the Spanish people to Cuba, an island in the West Indies. These 89 Native Americans lived in Cuba as Spanish citizens for the rest of their lives. The last Timucua man was named Juan Alonso Cabale. He died in Cuba in 1767.

WHAT ABOUT DISEASES? When Europeans and Africans came to the New World, they accidentally brought diseases with them. Some of these diseases, like smallpox and the plague, were killing lots of people in Europe. Native Americans didn't have any **immunities** against these diseases. Sometimes one out

> If you have an immunity to a sickness, it means that your body knows how to fight that sickness. Florida's early Native Americans didn't have any immunities against these new diseases. If someone caught one of these new diseases, they usually didn't get well.

of every three people in a village died from a disease like influenza. That means that if 90 people lived in the village, at least 30 would die. Often the grandparents and babies died first, because they were weaker. If all of the older people died, who would be left to remember the histories of the village? Who would advise the chief? Who would be the shaman and take care of the sick people? If the chief died, who would be in charge? Many villages didn't know who to turn to. They often looked to the Spanish missionaries for help in getting organized again.

Detective Directive 44: Look at figure Y. Each symbol stands for one person in a small village. Look at the key, then color each symbol with the correct color. Answer the questions below to find out what happened to Florida's Native Americans.

Figure Y. Why the Timucua disappeared

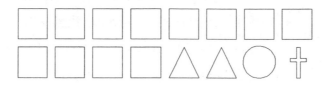

Grandmothers and grandfathers

Moms and dads

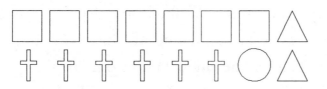

Kids

Key

△ Triangles were killed by Europeans who attacked Timucua villages. Color these red.

○ Circles were taken as slaves. Color these blue.

□ Squares were killed by diseases. Color these green.

☆ Stars were killed while protecting the missions and St. Augustine from the English. Color these purple.

✝ Crosses were taught about Christianity, so they lived as Spanish Catholics, not as Timucua. Some of these left Florida to go to Cuba in 1763. Color these orange.

*(1) What happened to most of the grandmothers
and grandfathers?*

_____

_____

(2) What two things happened to most of the kids?

_____

_____

(3) What is one way that only mothers and fathers usually died?

_____

*(4) How many Timucua from this village became Christian
Spanish citizens and stopped living like Timucua?* _____

☞   Cool Fact: After the last few Native Americans
     moved to Cuba with the Spanish, a few Timucua
     may have survived in hiding here in Florida. But
     they had to blend in with other cultures to survive.
     Their own Timucua culture (or way of life) was lost
     and forgotten. That's why we study them today, so
     they will never be forgotten completely.

13

Other Florida Native American Groups

Who Are the Seminole?

WHAT NATIVE AMERICAN NAMES ARE STILL USED IN THE SOUTHEAST TODAY? None of Florida's early Native American groups are alive today. Only their names are left behind.

 Detective Directive 45: Can you match the Native American name with the modern place? Draw lines to connect the correct names.

Native American name	A place named after it
Calusa	*Appalachian Mountains*
Yamassee	*Tampa, Florida*
Timucua	*Caloosahatchee River*
Apalachee	*Yemassee, South Carolina*
Tanpa, a Calusa village	*Tomoka River State Park*

☞ Cool Fact: Have you ever heard of the Suwannee River? There was a mission church for the Timucua near that river. It was called the St. Johns Mission. In Spanish, "St. John" is "San Juan." The Timucua called it "San Juanee." Later, this became "Suwannee."

WHO ARE THE SEMINOLE? After Florida's early Native Americans disappeared, the Seminole moved to Florida. The Seminole were originally Creek peoples, from Georgia and Alabama. The English were pushing them out of their homes, so they started coming to Florida in the 1700s. The name "Seminole" probably came from a Spanish word, *cimarrone*, which meant something like "renegade" or "Indian living away from a mission village."

In 1990, a government count said that there were over 36,000 Native Americans living in Florida, from 48 different cultural groups. If you want to know more about Native Americans today, there are lots of great books. Or you can check out the Internet. You can also meet some modern Native Americans at a powwow and ask them a few questions. Anything they tell you is called "oral history." Oral means "by mouth"—a story. You can learn from today's Native Americans in the same way Timucua kids learned from their grandparents.

14

Learning about the Past

What Is Archaeology?

HOW CAN WE LEARN ABOUT THE TIMUCUA? Because the Timucua are all gone, there are only two ways we can study about these Native Americans: the historical way and the archaeological way.

Using the HISTORIC method means reading the stories and studying the pictures left behind by the French, Spanish, and English. LeMoyne's pictures and Laudonnière's writings tell us many things. Also, the Spanish missionaries wrote many letters to the church about the Timucua. They even wrote the *Confessionario,* the main old book that tells us about the Timucua language. Studying these writings and pictures is a good way to study the past. This is called the HISTORIC method, because we learn from stories.

The other way we can study the past is called the ARCHAEOLOGICAL (ark-ee-oh-LOJ-i-cal) method. This is a way of studying the past by looking at actual things left behind. Archaeologists look at designs on old pottery, animal bones left in trash piles, and postholes left in the ground where huts had been. These things teach us about the kinds of tools, foods, and homes used by Native Americans long ago.

WHAT IS A BURIAL MOUND? A burial mound is a Native American cemetery. Today it is against the law to dig in a burial mound. The Timucua didn't put their dead in boxes and bury them in the ground. Instead, when a person died, they put the body on top of the ground. Then they covered it with dirt and maybe a layer of special clay. This is how the "mound" shape was made. (See figure Z.)

Sometimes, right after a person died, the body was put in a charnel (CHAR-nul) house. A long time later, the bones were gathered up and buried in the mound. This is called a "bundle burial." In figure Z, numbers 2, 3, 4, and 6 are bundle burials. When a person was buried right after death, it was called a "primary burial." In figure Z, numbers 1, 5, and 7 are primary burials.

Figure Z. How burial mounds are made

Dirt is piled up over the skeleton each time someone is buried. Can you see how a mound shape would form?

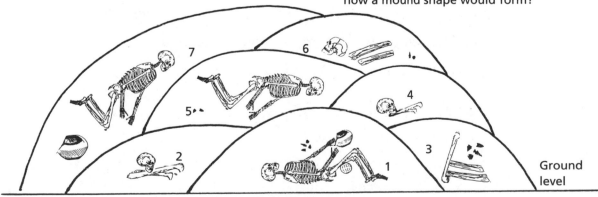

Ground level

Number 1 was buried first, then 2, then 3, and so on.

Sometimes people were buried with special things like pottery, weapons, or jewelry. These tools were usually broken before they were buried. The Timucua may have believed that breaking the pot or tool meant that it was "dead." Because these tools had been "killed," the dead person could take them to the spirit world. Some pots were even made with a piece missing, so they could be "dead" without being really broken.

WHAT IS A MIDDEN? In Florida, a midden is a trash pile left behind by Native Americans. Near a salt marsh, these middens are mostly made up of oyster shells. This is because oysters grow well in a salt marsh, and the Timucua ate a lot of oysters. Near a freshwater river, these middens are made mostly of snail shells. In other places, closer to the beach, clams, oysters, and whelk shells will be mixed together. There are even small middens made of coquina. These trash piles help us to learn what Florida's Native Americans ate. Mixed with these shells, archaeologists find deer bones, sharks' teeth, alligator scales, and many other animal parts. They also find broken pottery and tools, which teach us even more about the Timucua.

Detective Directive 46: On the next few pages, look at figures AA and BB. They show many things you could find in a Native American midden in Florida. Use figure AA to help you investigate what's in the "midden" in figure BB. What did you find in the midden? Write it below.

Animal parts
you found

1_____
2_____
3_____
4_____
5_____
6_____
7_____
8_____
9_____
10_____

Animals the
Timucua hunted

1_____
2_____
3_____
4_____
5_____
6_____
7_____
8_____
9_____

Other things

1_____
2_____

Figure AA. Things you could find in a Florida midden

Alligator jaw

Opossum jaw

Deer rib

Deer leg bone

Turtle shell

Alligator scale

Dolphin vertebra (backbone part)

Fish vertebra (backbone part)

Oyster shell

Deer skull

Raccoon skull

Whelk shell

Broken pottery (Deptford Check-Stamped, made 2,500 to 1,250 years ago)

Deer scapula (shoulder blade)

Broken pottery (fiber-tempered, made 4,000 to 2,500 years ago)

Pinellas projectile point (made 750 to 250 years ago)

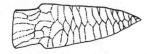

Columbia projectile point (made 1,800 to 750 years ago)

Clovis projectile point (made around 12,000 years ago)

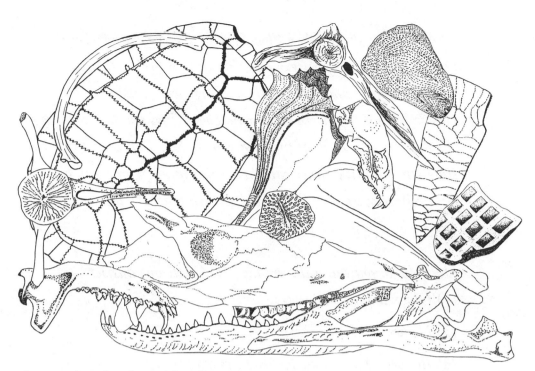

Figure BB. A Florida midden for you to excavate

Detective Directive 47: Archaeologists can tell how old a midden is by looking at the kinds of projectile points and pottery they find there. Look back at figures AA and BB. Think about the pottery timeline you saw earlier, on page 89. Then answer the questions on the next page to figure out how old this midden is.

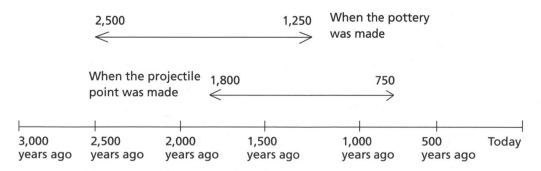

Archaeology Timeline

This timeline shows when Florida's Native Americans were making this kind of pottery and this kind of projectile point. Circle the time when both of these things were made. (Hint: Both things were made when both lines overlap, covering the same space.) Look at the area you circled. This is probably the time when Native Americans made this midden, or trash pile. An archaeologist can tell how old a trash pile is by looking at the pottery and projectile points in it.

How old do you think this midden is? Circle one answer.
(1) Older than 2,500 years

(2) Newer than 750 years

(3) Between 1,800 and 1,250 years old

☞ Cool Fact: Even if you are not a professional archaeologist, you can volunteer to go on digs and help scientists find historic and Native American artifacts. Colleges can usually tell you where to find an archaeologist to talk to.

Detective, you've completed your mission! You can use the next few pages to see how well you did.

If you'd like to find out more about the Native Americans of Florida and Georgia, be sure to check out the section called "Cool Ways for Kids to Learn about Native Americans." It lists a few books and lots of great parks and museums you can visit. It tells you what interesting things you will find at each place, too (like a giant prehistoric sloth skeleton, an Apalachee council house, or ancient projectile points).

There's also a section called "Further Reading for Adults" so your parents can learn more about Native Americans, too.

There are some great sites on the Web that you can learn from. Here's the address for a site I helped design. It has a whole "Timucua Kid Section." Visit the Pelotes Island Nature Preserve home page at http://pelotes.jea.com, or type in the keyword "Pelotes" or "Timucua."

Have fun learning. And try to remember the Timucua people forever!

Answers to Detective Directive Questions

Make a check mark next to the ones you got right. Then go on to the next section called "Congratulations to the Detective: How Did You Do?" If the question was something like "What is your favorite color?" then "your answer" is correct because that is your opinion. Everything marked "your answer" is automatically correct.

DD1 (p. 5): This one is for you to figure out!

DD2 (p. 7): Make an arrow across the ice bridge from Siberia to Alaska.

DD3 (p. 9): Make an arrow from Alaska to Florida. Go between the glaciers.

DD4 (p. 10): Draw an arrow from Spain to the West Indies.

DD5 (p. 13): This one is for you to figure out!

DD6 (p. 14): Color in the cross-hatch area; Ais, Apalachee, Calusa, Guale, Matecumbe, Tequesta.

DD7 (p. 15): Jacksonville = Timucua; Key West = Matecumbe; Miami = Tequesta; Orlando = Ais; Savannah = Guale; Tallahassee = Apalachee; Tampa = Calusa.

DD8 (p. 16): (1) chiri; (2) honoso; (3) honosoma; (4) tapolama; (5) ticoma; (6) ticosi; (7) hasomisi; (8) atulusi; (9) hontala ihiribi; (10) hontala chirisi.

DD9 (p. 21): Because the French were so short, it made the Timucua seem really tall!

DD10 (p. 25): This one is for you to figure out!

DD11 (p. 26): Your answer; no; maybe none of the girls in your class like to wear braids, but some girls in the next classroom may like to; no; maybe in another village they did wear braids.

DD12 (p. 27): Your answer; your answer; girls.

DD13 (p. 28): It could protect his heart and lungs from a spear.

DD14 (p. 29): No; no; on special occasions.

DD15 (p. 30): This one is for you to figure out!

DD16 (p. 31): The people with the most tattoos would be the chief's family. In this picture, they are the man with the chief's stick and the woman with the flower.

DD17 (p. 33): (1) Girls. (2) Boys. (3) Married. (4) Moms and dads. (5) Kids. (6) Brothers and sisters. (7) No; married people aren't in the same clan, and you can't cross an = sign; yes. (8) Yes. (9) No; don't cross an = sign. (10) No; no. (11) Mom, uncle #4, aunt #5. (12) Married people aren't in the same clan; don't cross the = sign. (13) Married people aren't in the same clan; don't cross the = sign; yes. (14) Yes; no; married people aren't in the same clan. (15) Brother #6, brother #7, sister #8. (16) Yes. (17) No. (18) These people are in your Timucua clan: great-grandmother, grandmother #2, great-uncle, aunt #3, cousin #3a, cousin #3b, uncle #4, aunt #5, cousin #5a, cousin #5b, mom, brother #6, brother #7, sister #8, nephew #8, niece #8, you.

DD18 (p. 42): No. Men hunt large animals, teach boys, build huts, make canoes, protect village, make weapons. Women teach girls, collect fruits and nuts, grind corn, cook meat, weave baskets, make pottery, cure skins into leather, sew clothes, make medicines, carry water to village, care for kids, work in fields, hunt small animals, make big decisions. The clan helps to build huts, make canoes, plant and harvest gardens, take care of orphans. The women do the most work.

DD19 (p. 44): Kids today.

DD20 (p. 46): A foot race; a canoe race; archery (shooting arrows); a ball game.

DD21 (p. 46): Yes; it trains their arms to throw a spear.

DD22 (p. 48): It helped them to swim longer underwater.

DD23 (p. 48): When you try to follow, find, and catch other kids, it's like hunting and tracking animals.

DD24 (p. 48): Arm wrestle; play ball; build sand castles; canoe; climb trees; dance; play tag; go on dates; do gymnastics; play hide and seek; play leap frog; listen to music; build forts; play with dolls; have foot races; have splash fights; have swim races.

DD25 (p. 52): One; your answer; your answer; modern Floridians have more space; your answer; your answer (but rather be outside in the fresh air).

DD26 (p. 53): So they could see dangerous animals coming too close.

DD27 (p. 56): Fence; yes.

DD28 (p. 57): Rectangle; yes.

DD29 (p. 58): This one is for you to figure out!

DD30 (p. 60): To clear away weeds; ash makes good fertilizer.

DD31 (p. 62): Sweetgum; any of these vegetables: cabbage heart, prickly pear, dandelion leaves, mushrooms; any of these spices: bay leaves, saltwort, wax myrtle.

DD32 (p. 63): You can have any of the following answers for each part of the meal.

Teas: pine needles, goldenrod flowers, winged sumac's lemony fruits, horsemint, yaupon holly leaves (to make the black drink—for male ceremonies only), and many more.

Crops: corn, squash, pumpkins, sunflowers, and peas.

Fruits: grapes, blueberries, blackberries, plums, persimmons, and many more.

Cooked vegetable: onions, cabbage palm heart, prickly pear, dandelion leaves, mushrooms, and many more.

Bread: acorns, hickory nuts, cattail roots and flowers, chinquapin nuts, pigweed, wild rice, and many more.

Water animal: alligators, clams, crabs, crayfish, ducks and their eggs, fish, marine mammals, mussels, oysters, sharks, shrimp, and turtles and their eggs.

Land animal: bears, bird eggs, deer, opossums, rabbits, raccoons, snakes, squirrels, tortoises and their eggs, turkeys, and wild pigs (after the Europeans brought pigs to Florida).

Seasonings: bay leaves, peppergrass seeds, saltwort, wax myrtle, and many more.

DD33 (p. 66): You can cook your meal any of these ways.

Teas: boiling fresh or dried plants.

Vegetables: boiled.

Bread: nuts and grains were pounded into flour, made into dough, and baked as bread, fried as fritters, or boiled as dumplings.

Fruits: eaten fresh, made into jelly, or dried in the sun.

Corn: raw or cooked; dried hard and pounded into grits or corn flour to make bread.

Seeds: eaten raw or cooked.

Meats and fish: meats were roasted over a fire, cooked in a stew, or dried into jerky. Some shellfish, like oysters and whelks, could be eaten raw, steamed over a fire, or cooked into a stew.

DD34 (p. 66): Deer, alligator, snake, fish, fox; no.

DD35 (p. 67): Meat and fish: dried fish, dried deer meat. Fruits and vegetables: palm cabbage, peppergrass, blueberry jelly. Carbohy-drates: acorn bread, grits, wild rice. Your answer; your answer.

DD36 (p. 71): Ground-cherry leaves; buttonbush.

DD37 (p. 78): (1) Bow and arrow, spear, club. (2) No. (3) No; no. (4) No; loincloth. (5) No.

DD38 (p. 82): Man; older; fire it to make it harder, which turns it pink; to hunt.

DD39 (p. 86): Swift Creek (Timucua); St. Johns Plain (Timucua); St. Johns Check-Stamped (Timucua); Deptford Check-Stamped (Timucua); Orange Period (not Timucua). Your answer.

DD40 (p. 90): (1) Antlers used for tools to make arrowheads, knife handles. (2) Meat used for food. (3) Gourds used for buckets, scoops, bowls. (4) Stomachs used for water bags. (5) Cypress used for canoes. (6) Rivercane used for arrow or spear shaft. (7) Shells and animal bones used for bowls, axes, hoes, jewelry, needles, whistles, flutes, knives, fishhooks. (8) Hickory used for bows, canoe paddles. (9) Hides used for clothes, bowstrings, blankets, packs. (10) Chert stone used for projectile points, knives, drills. (11) Clay used for pottery, pipes.

DD41 (p. 92): This one is for you to figure out!

DD42 (p. 98): Bad; good; bad; bad; wood; back.

DD43 (p. 102): Slow; no; there isn't any gold here; no; yes; from the Apalachee people; no. (1) No, there is no gold in Florida; also a flat basket would work better than a pole for getting gold out of water. (2) No; we know there's no gold in Florida, so we know that picture is false. (3) No; there's no archaeological proof for fences around villages. (4) No, there is some true stuff; there is archaeological proof for round Timucua homes.

DD44 (p. 107): (1) Disease. (2) Disease and learned about Christianity (went to Cuba). (3) Killed protecting the missions and St. Augustine. (4) Nine.

DD45 (p. 110): Calusa = Caloosahatchee River; Yamasee = Yemassee, South Carolina; Timucua = Tomoka River State Park; Apalachee = Appalachian Mountains; Tanpa = Tampa, Florida.

DD46 (p. 115): Animal parts found: scapula, rib, vertebra, turtle shell, skull, oyster shell, whelk shell, scale, jaw, leg. Animals: deer, tortoise (land turtle), alligator, raccoon, dolphin, oyster, opossum, fish, whelk. Other: Columbia projectile point, Deptford Check-Stamped pottery.

DD47 (p. 117): (3) Between 1,800 and 1,250 years old.

Congratulations to the Detective: How Did You Do?

WELL, DETECTIVE, HOW DID YOU DO? Count the number of marks you put next to correct answers. Write that number here: _____ This is how many answers you got right.

If you got fewer than 24 answers right, try reading the book again. You're sure to do better next time! You can cut out the ribbon in figure CC and write "Junior Archaeologist" on the circle. Color the rest of your ribbon green.

If you got 25 to 34 answers correct, you're well on your way to becoming a historical detective! You can cut out the ribbon in figure CC and write "Archaeologist—D.I.T." on the circle. (That means "Archaeologist—Detective in Training.") Color the rest of your ribbon yellow.

If you got 34 to 40 correct, you probably know more about the Timucua than most grown-ups do! You're ready to start training others and doing detective work on your own. Cut out the ribbon in figure CC and write "Archaeology

Detective" on the circle. Color the rest of your ribbon red.

If you got 40 to 47 correct, you are a master historical detective! Cut out the ribbon in figure CC and write "Archaeology Detective Extraordinaire" on the circle. You know everything in this book. So find a new book and keep investigating. Color the rest of your ribbon blue and wear it with pride!

Write your score and your new title on this line.

_____

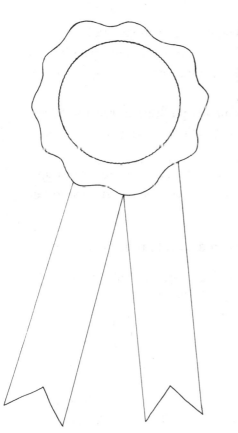

Congratulations to all of you for a job well done! With future historical detectives like you, we'll be learning more about the Timucua and other Native American groups every day.

Figure CC. Detective's ribbon

Cool Ways for Kids to Learn about Native Americans

Check Out These Books!

Florida's First People, by Robin Brown, is a book for grown-ups, but it tells how to do all sorts of interesting things, like making a canoe, weaving Spanish moss cloth, and curing an animal hide. It has great pictures and explanations, because Mr. Brown tried all of these things himself!

Keepers of the Animals, by Michael Caduto and Joseph Bruchac, has true Native American stories and wildlife activities for kids. Michael Caduto is the best storyteller I've ever met.

A Foothold in Florida, by John Faupel and Sara Lawson, is a book for grown-ups, but it has lots of pictures of the Timucua people. It also contains stories written down by the French soldier Laudonnière.

Places in Florida and Georgia to Learn about Native Americans

The Florida-Georgia region is split up into five areas: the Panhandle (Northwest Florida), Northeast Florida, Central Florida, South Florida, and Georgia. There are places in each area where you can have fun learning about Native Americans. Look on the Internet for more.

Panhandle

Lake Jackson Mounds. You can hike all over Apalachee mounds. These aren't middens; they're actually high places the Apalachee built for the chief, the shaman, and as burial houses.

3600 Indian Mound Road

Tallahassee, FL 32303

(850) 922-6007

Museum of Florida History has murals of Archaic peoples and Paleoindians and lots of artifacts to see. You can also see the spot where the Spanish soldiers camped when they met Florida's Native Americans over 400 years ago.

500 South Bronough Street

Tallahassee, FL 32399-0250

(850) 488-1484

San Luis Archaeological Site. The spot where an Apalachee council house once stood is marked. A Spanish mission church and a Spanish house have been rebuilt, and they're starting to rebuild the council house and the chief's house, too. Check out their museum and the huge yaupon holly hedge while you are there.

2020 West Mission Road

Tallahassee, FL 32304

(850) 487-3711

Northeast Florida

Castillo de San Marcos. You can explore the actual fort in St. Augustine. It was built by the Spanish in the 1600s. (The Timucua helped build it, too.) If you climb around in the old coquina fort, you can see the moat and the old Spanish guns.

1 South Castillo Drive

St. Augustine, FL 32084

(904) 829-6506

Florida Museum of Natural History has a great exhibit on Florida's Native Americans, with a thatched hut you can walk into and life-sized murals of Native peoples.

Powell Hall

University of Florida

Box 112710

Gainesville, FL 32611-2710

(352) 846-2967

Fort Caroline National Memorial has some exhibits on Florida's Native Americans and the French, nature trails, and a replica of the French-built Fort Caroline. Nearby you can see a copy of the French Ribault Monument. The rangers there will tell you about the Timucua people when you visit.

12713 Fort Caroline Road

Jacksonville, FL 32225

(904) 641-7155

Heritage of the Ancient Ones. A native village has been re-created for you to explore, and workshops teach about native tool-making and pottery-making. Phone for reservations.

625 Theodore Street

St. Augustine, FL 32095

(904) 824-3325

Jacksonville Museum of Science and History. Check out the "Currents of Time" exhibit to see Timucua artifacts, including projectile points (arrowheads), and displays on Florida's Native Americans and its Spanish and French settlers.

1025 Museum Circle

Jacksonville, FL 32207

(904) 396-7062

Morningside Nature Center has a nature walk and a place to try Native American gardening, music-making, and rope-weaving. A life-sized thatched hut is being built, too.

3540 East University Avenue

Gainesville, FL 32641

(352) 334-2170

Museum of Arts and Sciences at Daytona Beach has an exhibit with a 12-foot-tall prehistoric sloth skeleton that shows how the Paleoindians hunted this giant animal. There are also Timucua tools and jewelry, a model of a burial mound, and two copies of totem poles. Their newest exhibit has touch-screen computers showing Florida history from the Paleoindians right up to today.

1040 Museum Blvd.

Daytona Beach, FL 32114

(904) 255-0285

Paynes Prairie State Park features a visitors' center with Native American displays.

Route 2, Box 41

Micanopy, FL 32667

(352) 466-3397

Pelotes Island Nature Preserve has a life-sized Timucua hut and lots of native trash middens to hike over. Learn about the Timucua by trying archaeology or learning native skills and games.

Pelotes Island

11201 New Berlin Road

Jacksonville, FL 32226

(904) 665-8856

http://pelotes.jea.com

Silver River Museum has a real mammoth skeleton and a giant shark jaw. Murals show how Native Americans hunted mammoths. In fact, a mammoth skeleton and lots of projectile points were found right next to the museum. There are also displays of real Native American tools and points from the Paleoindians up to the Seminole.

1445 NE 58th Avenue

Ocala, FL 34470

(352) 236-5401

Talbot Islands State Parks have shell middens shaped in giant rings.

12157 Heckscher Drive

Jacksonville, FL 32226

(904) 251-2320

Theodore Roosevelt Area of the Timucua Preserve. There are 30 acres of middens here to hike over.

12713 Fort Caroline Road

Jacksonville, FL 32225

(904) 221-5568.

Tomoka River State Park has projectile points here to check out and recent paintings that show what the Timucua people might have looked like.

2099 North Beach Street

Ormand Beach, FL 32174

(904) 676-4050

Central Florida

Bobby's Seminole Indian Village. You can check out a Seminole village, alligator wrestlers, and a museum that tells all about the history of the Seminole people.

5221 North Orient Road

Tampa, FL 33610

(813) 620-3077

Brevard Museum of History and Natural Sciences has three exhibits on Native Americans, a hands-on fossil exhibit, and 22 acres of nature trails. You can check out artifacts and life-sized mannequins showing how the Seminole people looked and how Native Americans were buried at the Windover archaeological site over 7,000 years ago.

2201 Michigan Avenue

Cocoa, FL 32926

(407) 632-1830

Canaveral National Seashore. Here you can hike over large middens made of oyster, whelk, and clam shells. There are Native American tools to look at and a video to watch, too.

7611 South Atlantic Avenue (A1A Highway)

New Smyrna Beach, FL 32169

(904) 428-3384

Crystal River State Archaeological Site. There are mounds here built by Native Americans between 200 B.C. and 1400 A.D. Trail markers throughout the mounds tell how the Native Americans used their habitat. There's also a museum with lots of information on archaeology and the Native Americans who lived there.

3400 North Museum Point

Crystal River, FL 34428

(352) 795-3817

Fort Christmas Historical Museum and Parks. Here you can learn all about the Seminole wars. An 1837 Seminole war fort has been rebuilt, and there are Native American artifacts on display, too.

1300 Fort Christmas Road

Christmas, FL 32079

(407) 568-4149

Hontoon Island State Park. Some totem poles were found near here. At the nature museum, you can see copies of the owl and otter totems. You can also hike midden trails and go camping, fishing, and biking.

2309 River Ridge Road

Deland, FL 32720

(904) 736-5309

Manatee River Basin Geo-Park. Here you will find the Madira Bickel Mound State Archaeological Site—a 20-foot-high ceremonial mound made of shell and sand. You can hike all the way to the top!

3708 Patten Avenue

Ellenton, FL 34222

(941) 723-4536

Orange County Historical Museum. There is a dugout canoe on display and lots of Native American artifacts to check out.

812 East Rollins Street

Orlando, FL 32803

(407) 897-6350

Seminole Student Museum has a whole room set up like a Timucua village with a hut, a canoe, a meat-drying rack, and a mural scene on all four walls. The museum staff can tell you a lot about Florida's Native Americans.

301 Seventh Street

Sanford, FL 32711–2505

(407) 320-0502

South Florida Museum. Murals show prehistoric animals and Native Americans, and you can see artifacts from the Timucua and other cultures.

201 10th Street West

Bradenton, FL 34205

(941) 746-4131

South Florida

Arch Creek Midden. This spot has almost five acres of clam- and oyster-shell middens laid down by the Tequesta Indians between 2,500 and 700 years ago. A small museum shows the artifacts found here. You can also check out the Tequesta Nature Trail with a guidebook or a tour guide.

Arch Creek Park

1855 Northeast 135th Street

North Miami, FL 33161

(305) 944-6111

Calusa Coast Outfitters offer a summer Calusa Camp. Kids hike over the shell mounds at Mound Key, design shell tools, and make pottery, ceremonial masks, and cloth. They learn about Calusa foods and hunting, and they study archaeology. This company also gives tours of Mound Key to adults and families.

289 Connecticut Street

Fort Myers Beach, FL 33931

(941) 765-0865

Calusa Nature Center and Planetarium has trails through cypress swamps and Native American huts for you to explore.

3450 Ortiz Avenue

Fort Myers, FL 33905

(941) 275-3435

Georgia

Etowah Indian Mounds State Historic Site has three mounds to explore and a museum with over 400 artifacts. There is a real native fish trap in the river, too.

    813 Indian Mounds Road

    Cartersville, GA 30120

    (770) 387-3747

Fort King George State Historic Site. This museum displays artifacts from the Guale Indians, including a dugout canoe, pottery, and small statues. There's also a life-sized painting of a Guale Indian and a painting of what the Guale village there looked like. Displays show how the Guale changed when they met the Spanish.

    P.O. Box 711

    Darien, GA 31305

    (912) 437-4770

Kolomoki Mounds State Park. There are seven ceremonial mounds here, and you can climb stairs to the top of the highest—56 feet off the ground. One burial mound is partially excavated so you can see the skeletons and the things buried with them.

    Route 1

    Blakely, GA 31723

    (912) 723-5296

Ocmulgee National Monument. Here you can visit a burial/temple mound and explore an old Native American earth lodge. There is also a museum with projectile points, a native headdress, and Native American pipes.

    1207 Emery Highway

    Macon, GA 31201

    (912) 752-8257

Sapelo Island National Estuarine Research Reserve. A giant shell ring was built here by Native Americans long ago. You can take a guided tour to see it.

    P.O. Box 15

    Sapelo Island, GA 31327

    (912) 437-3224

Further Reading for Adults

Grown-up readers: Each picture noted in the text as a LeMoyne/ DeBry engraving has a long history. The Frenchman Jacques LeMoyne du Morgues drew pictures of the Timucua during his 1564 visit to Florida. Although most of his drawings were destroyed in a Spanish attack on Fort Caroline, he was able to redraw them from memory. After LeMoyne's death, Theodore DeBry received permission to engrave this set of drawings. He published them in Frankfurt in a Latin text called *Brevis narratio eorum quae in Florida Americae Provincia*. . . . Despite their many errors, these engravings have provided our best pictorial evidence of the Timucua culture since their publication in 1519.

Check out our reference list to learn more about the Timucua.

Ashley, Keith, and Bob Richter. *Excavation of the Dent Mound (8Du68), Duval County, Florida*. Jacksonville: Jacksonville Museum of Science and History, 1993.

Brown, Robin C. *Florida's First People*. Sarasota: Pineapple Press, 1994.

Brunn, Bertel, Chandler Robbins, and Herbert Zim. *A Golden Guide to Field Identification: Birds of North America*. Racine, Wis.: Western Publishing, 1983.

Bullen, Ripley P. *A Guide to the Identification of Florida Projectile Points*. Gainesville: Kendall Books, 1975.

Burrage, D. D. *Early English Voyages, 1534–1608.* New York: 1906.

Caduto, Michael J., and Joseph Bruchac. *Keepers of the Animals.* Golden, Colo.: Fulcrum Publishing, 1991.

Cotterill, R. S. *The Southern Indians: The Story of the Civilized Tribes before Removal.* Norman: University of Oklahoma Press, 1989.

Culberson, Linda Crawford. *Arrowheads and Spear Points in the Prehistoric Southeast.* Jackson: University Press of Mississippi, 1993.

Dobyns, Henry F. *Their Number Becoming Thinned.* Knoxville: University of Tennessee Press, 1983.

Duke, James A., and Stephen Foster. *Peterson Field Guides: Eastern/Central Medicinal Plants.* Boston: Houghton Mifflin, 1990.

Faupel, W. John, and Sarah Lawson. *A Foothold in Florida.* East Grinstead, Eng.: Antique Atlas Publications, 1992.

Flint Knapping with Bruce Bradley, Ph.D. A video produced by INTERpark and Primitive Technology Graphics, 1989.

Hudson, Charles. *The Southeastern Indians.* Knoxville: University of Tennessee Press, 1976.

———, ed. *Black Drink: A Native American Tea.* Athens: University of Georgia Press, 1979.

Hudson, Charles, and Carmen Chaves Tesser, eds. *The Forgotten Centuries: Indians and Europeans in the American South, 1521–1704.* Athens: University of Georgia Press, 1994.

Kelley, Todd, living historian. Interview. Jacksonville, Fla., 1995.

Milanich, Jerald T. *Archaeology of Precolumbian Florida.* Gainesville: University Press of Florida, 1994.

———. *Florida Indians and the Invasion from Europe.* Gainesville: University Press of Florida, 1995.

———. *The Timucuas.* Oxford, Eng., and Cambridge, Mass.: Blackwell, 1996.

Milanich, Jerald T., and Susan Milbrath, eds. *First Encounters: Spanish Explorations in the Caribbean and the United States, 1492–1570.* Gainesville: University of Florida Press, 1990.

Milanich, Jerald T., and Samuel Proctor, eds. *Tacachale: Essays on the Indians of Florida and Southeastern Georgia during the Historic Period.* Gainesville: University of Florida Press, 1978.

Milanich, Jerald T., and William C. Sturtevurt. *Francisco Pareja's 1613 "Confessionario": A Documentary Source for Timucuan Ethnography.* Tallahassee: Division of Archives, History, and Records Management, Florida Department of State, 1978.

Morris, Craig, park ranger, Timucuan Ecological and Historic Preserve, National Park Service. Interview. Jacksonville, 1995.

Peterson, Lee Allen. *Peterson Field Guides: Edible Wild Plants.* Boston: Houghton Mifflin, 1977.

Seminole Student Museum, Sanford, Fla. Interview, staff member, 1995.

Snow, Dean R. *The Iroquois.* Oxford, Eng., and Cambridge, Mass.: Blackwell, 1994.

Ste. Claire, Dana. *True Natives: The Prehistory of Volusia County.* Daytona Beach, Fla.: Hall Publishing, 1992.

Stokes, Donald, and Lillian Stokes. *A Guide to Animal Tracking and Behavior.* Boston: Little, Brown, 1986.

Walton, Richard K., and Robert W. Lawson. *Peterson Field Guides: Eastern/Central Birding by Ear.* Boston: Houghton Mifflin, 1989.

Whitaker, John O., Jr. *Audubon Society Field Guide to North American Mammals.* New York: Alfred A. Knopf, Chanticleer Press, 1980.

Glossary: What Do All Those Words Mean?

archaeologist (ar-kee-OL-oh-jist): A scientist who investigates things like tools and pottery that were made by people long ago. He or she tries to discover what life was like for ancient people.

caffeine (ka-FEEN): A chemical in a lot of sodas, coffees, and teas that tricks your body into thinking you're not tired. When you drink something with caffeine, your body makes a survival (fight-or-flight) chemical, and you feel a little hyperactive. Caffeine does not give you any extra energy. Since your body was already tired before you started feeling this way, you feel really run down when there is no more caffeine in your system. Today, having a caffeine drink before a race or game is not the best way to prepare for a good performance. A sports drink, a piece of fruit, or a good meal of carbohydrates like pasta helps you more.

carbohydrate (car-bo-HI-drate): A high-energy food, like bread, rice, spaghetti, nuts, or corn. The Timucua probably didn't have spaghetti, but they could eat all of these other foods to get energy for a hunt, a day of gardening, a fishing trip, or an exciting game of hide-and-seek.

chert: This white rock is the only stone in Florida that is good for making tools. It is not as good as flint, but there isn't much flint in Florida. The Timucua had to use what they could find. Since there wasn't much chert in Florida either, many Florida Native Americans used shells for their tools instead.

clan: A group of people who are related to each other because they all share a common ancestor. An ancestor can be a grandmother, or a great-great-great-great-grandfather, depending on what kind of clan you are in. Among the Timucua, the common ancestor would have to be a woman, because they were matrilineal, a mother-line clan.

clay: A smooth type of dirt that is slimy and easy to squeeze into shapes when it is wet. It can be found in the bottoms of some streams and rivers and sometimes under the ground. Baking clay in a fire makes it hard and dry.

club: A wooden tool that looks a little like a baseball bat. It could be used in hunting or in battle.

corn: A very important plant for the Timucua. They grew corn in their gardens by soaking kernels in water, then planting them in little hills of dirt. Since the weather is so warm in Florida, there is a really long growing season. The Timucua could plant corn twice. One kind, called "early corn," was planted in the spring and picked in the summer. They ate it raw or boiled. "Late corn" was planted in the summer and harvested late in the fall. The corn dried hard on the plant. Later, the dry corn kernels were pounded into grits or corn flour. Corn flour was used to make flat cornbread. Some hard kernels were saved to be used as seeds next year.

culture (ᴋᴜʟ-chur): A way of life. Your culture includes the kind of foods you eat, your clothes, your music, your religion, your language, your games and dances, and everything else that makes your people special and different from others.

cure: A way of making sure an animal skin, or hide, does not rot. Cured animal skin is called "leather." See the definition of "leather" to learn how the Timucua cured, or tanned, animal skins into leather for clothing.

detective (dee-ᴛᴇᴋ-tiv): A person who discovers the truth. Detectives investigate facts and stories to figure out what really happened.

directive (di-ʀᴇᴋ-tiv): Something you want to accomplish; an order or challenge to complete a task.

dye: A kind of paint or stain. The Timucua made dyes from leaves, berries, stems, and more. They might crush an acorn and soak it in water to release its brownish-orange color. Then they could dip leather into the brown water to color the leather brown. They may have mixed wood ashes and berry juice to rub into tattoo needle marks to give the tattoo a color. Today people make dyes out of many different things.

engrave (en-ɢʀᴀᴠᴇ): To cut or scratch a design into wood or metal. LeMoyne drew pictures of the Timucua with pen and paper. DeBry wanted to put the pictures in a book. In those days, there were no copy machines. To make copies of pictures for a book, you had to cut the lines of each picture into a piece of wood or metal, then dip that in ink. All the extra ink was wiped off. Then, when you pressed the inky metal on paper, it left an imprint of the picture. You *had* to engrave a picture if you wanted to make lots of copies. Sometimes an engraved picture was not exactly like the drawing.

Europeans (yur-oh-PEE-unz): People from Europe. Europe is across the Atlantic Ocean from the United States. There are many countries in Europe. In the 1500s, the three main European countries that sent people to the east coast of North America were Spain, France, and England.

extinct (ex-TINKT): What you call a type of animal or plant or a group of people that have died out. Once there were large animals like mastodons (giant hairy elephants), camels, giant armadillos, and horses in Florida. About 10,000 years ago all of these big animals started to die out. There were no horses in Florida after that, so the Timucua didn't have any animals to ride. In the 1500s, the Spanish brought horses from Europe. That's why we have horses today.

fish bladder (fish BLA-dur): A tiny air sac inside a fish that helps it float underwater. The French said that the Timucua made fish bladders into ear decorations.

glacier (GLAY-sher): Giant sheet of ice up to a mile thick. These ice sheets were made by nature from snow and frozen water. They covered much of Canada and some of the United States, too. Glaciers still cover other northern countries. Plants don't grow on glaciers, so they are not good places for people or animals to live. When the Paleoindians were crossing the Bering land bridge, they walked between the big ice sheets, not on them.

harvest (HAR-vest): The time when the corn, beans, squash, and pumpkins in the village garden are ripe, and people pick them to use for food. Usually a whole village works together to harvest the crops.

head chief: Each small Timucua village had a chief. All of the villages who were friendly with each other had one leader, called a "head chief." The head chief made important decisions for all of the villages. One head chief could rule 30 or more villages.

honey and honeybees (HUN-ee-bees): European honeybees were brought to this country from Europe, probably by the Spanish in the 1500s. Bees are insects that visit flowers to collect two things: pollen and nectar. Pollen is a good food for them and their babies, and it has lots of protein. They collect nectar (plant sugar water) to get its sugary energy. Bees change the nectar into honey. They store it in their hives as a winter food. When the Timucua got honey from a hive, they always left enough for the bees to eat.

immunities (i-MYOON-i-tees): Having immunities against a disease means your body knows how to fight that disease. The Native Americans didn't have any immunities against European and African diseases like smallpox and the plague. Many Timucua died from diseases like these. If they did get well, they would have immunities for that *one* disease. Unfortunately, this did not protect them from all the *other* new diseases. (After YOU get chicken pox once, your body makes immunities. You probably won't ever get it again.)

Indonesia (in-do-NEE-zhuh): A group of islands southeast of China which has many names, like the "East Indies" and the "Spice Islands." These islands were famous for the food spices their people grew and sold. People who wanted to buy the spices had to make a long, dangerous journey across land or sail around the tip of Africa to get there. Columbus was trying to find a faster, safer, cheaper way to get there by going across the ocean around the other side of the world. Instead, he bumped into the West Indies, just southeast of Florida. Some of the many small islands in Indonesia are Sumatra, Java, Sulawesi, the Moluccas, parts of Borneo, New Guinea, and Timor.

interview (IN-tur-vyoo): Asking a person questions so that you can learn what he or she knows. When you interview someone, always take good notes so that you can remember everything that is said. Each word might be important!

knapping (NAP-ing): The way that Timucua people made stone tools. They used an antler hammer to knock pieces off a chunk of chert stone. Then they would take a small deer antler and break tiny chips off the stone tool until it was complete. It takes years to learn the skill of knapping stone tools.

leather (LEH-thur): Animal hide (skin) that has had the fur taken off. It has been treated with a process called "curing" or "tanning," which stops the hide from rotting. The Timucua used brain-tanning to preserve their leather and furs. They probably dried the animal's brain, ground it into a powder, and mixed it with water. Then they rubbed the liquid into the animal hide and hung the hide over a really smoky fire. This process made the leather or fur soft and clean; and it would never rot. Today factories use chemicals to treat leather. Leather is usually made from cows' hides today. Some people wear shoes and coats made out of leather. These leather clothes keep people warm today, just as deer leather clothes kept the Timucua warm long ago.

matrilineal (ma-tri-LIN-ee-ul): "Mother line." The Timucua were a matrilineal people. They figured out who their relatives were by tracing their line through mothers, grandmothers, and great-grandmothers. It helped them to know who was in their clan.

midden (MID-den): A trash pile. Timucua trash piles contained mostly shells like oyster, whelk, clam, and snail. Animal bones and parts, broken pottery, and broken projectile points are also found in middens.

mission (MISS-shun): A place where one or two friars or priests lived and taught Florida's Native Americans about Christianity.

monument (MON-u-ment): A big stone column that might have a sign or picture on it. The French monument had a big *fleur-de-lis* (flur-de-LEE) on it, a flower that is the sign of France.

oyster (OY-stur): A small sea animal, like a clam, with two hard, white shells to keep it safe. Oysters have no way of moving themselves around; they're just stuck in one place. If a tiny bit of sand gets inside their shells, it really bothers them. They make a smooth, shiny material called "mother of pearl" to cover the sand over and over until it can't annoy them anymore. That little bit of sand becomes an oyster pearl. The Timucua gathered pearls from oysters.

poisonous (POY-sonus): Something that can make you sick or kill you if you eat it. Some plants have poisons in their leaves, fruits, and roots to keep people and animals from eating them. The poisons help keep the plant safe. Some animals can eat plants that people can't eat, because their stomachs are different from people's stomachs. Just because you see an animal eating a plant does NOT mean it's safe for you to eat. Never eat a wild plant. It could be poisonous!

poultice (POLE-tis): A paste made of mashed medicine plants. They may be mixed with grain or clay and are often heated. The warm mixture is put directly on an injury and tied with a bandage. The warmth and the plant's medicine help the injury to heal.

projectile (pro-JEK-tile) point: A handmade tool, such as an arrowhead, spearhead, or knife, is known by scientists today as a "projectile point." Such tools can be made of chert stone, sharks' teeth, fish spines, wood, bones, and many other things.

quest: An expedition or journey to find or learn new things.

research (ree-SEARCH): Finding the answer to a question or learning more about a subject by doing experiments, looking things up in the library, or asking an expert questions.

responsibilities (ree-spon-si-BILL-i-tees): Important jobs you must do so that everyone is cared for and kept safe.

ruby (ROO-bee): A precious stone with a deep red color. Today rubies are made into jewelry.

Siberia (si-BEER-ee-uh): A cold place in northern Russia. Today a small strip of water mostly separates Russia from North America. This is called the Bering Strait. During the last Ice Age, much of the ocean's water was frozen into glaciers. This made the dry ocean bottom stick up in some places. One place was at the Bering Strait. During the Ice Age, Siberia was attached to North America by a strip of ocean bottom called the Bering land bridge. Paleoindians followed herds of animals across this land bridge thousands of years ago. After a lot of walking, they arrived in North America.

smudge fire: A small fire the Timucua lit under their sleeping benches. Because the flames were very small, the fires did not burn down the hut. Instead, these little smudge fires made smoke. This smoke kept bugs away from the sleeping people, so they didn't get bitten at night.

snare: A trap for catching animals. It has a loop that tightens up when an animal runs through it. This usually kills or really hurts the animal badly, so you should never put out a snare just for fun.

Spanish moss: A plant with curly greenish-gray leaves which grows in tree branches. It is not a true moss but is actually related to a pineapple! Spanish moss does not steal food from the tree. Instead, it uses the tree as a ladder to help it reach sunlight. When moss grows close to the ground, or dies and falls to the ground, red bugs (or chiggers) can get into it. If you play with the moss, these tiny bugs can get on you and make you itch. If this happens, don't put nail polish on the bites; that doesn't help. Instead, use itch medicine, and try not to scratch the bites. The best thing to do is stay away from the moss. Timucua women used Spanish moss to make a rough gray cloth. They must have boiled the moss to kill the red bugs. Or maybe they put it near a really smoky fire, because bugs don't like smoke. They must have done something to get rid of the bugs—no one likes to itch!

spear-thrower: The longer your arms are, the farther you can throw a spear. A spear-thrower is a tool that works like a long arm. It's a long piece of wood to hold in your hand, and you hook a spear to the end of it. Then when you throw the spear, it's like you have a really long arm, and your spear goes far! A spear-thrower is also called an "atlatl" (at-LAT-ul).

status (STA-tus): How important you are and how much responsibility you have. The chief and the chief's family had very high status, and so did a great warrior. Very young hunters probably did not have much status, because they had not yet had a chance to prove how brave and talented they were.

superstition (soo-per-STI-shun): A belief that cannot be proven by science or fact. For example, some people believe that eating chicken soup can help a sick person get well sooner.

There aren't many facts to prove this, but lots of people believe it.

tattoo (ta-TOO): A permanent mark that some grown-ups put on their skin with needles. Getting a tattoo is a very serious grown-up decision for three reasons: it can hurt a lot; real tattoos don't wipe off once you get them; and sometimes you can accidentally get really bad germs from getting a tattoo. The Timucua got tattoos with bone needles. Sometimes this made them sick, because germs would get into the holes they poked in their skin. They made designs on their skin with the needle marks, then rubbed wood ashes and sometimes berry juice into the holes to leave a mark. The wood ashes helped to stop germs. The more important you were in the village, the more tattoos you had. This showed your status.

thatch: A way of making a roof from plants. Timucua homes used palm leaves (fronds), woven over and under other branches and grapevines. These made a tight, waterproof roof.

tobacco (toe-BACK-oh): A plant used today to make cigarettes. Now we know that tobacco can cause cancer, but the Timucua did not know this.

translation (tranz-LAY-shun): Changing a story from one language into another language, like from Spanish to English. A story may change a little bit when it is translated, just as it does when several people tell a story to each other without writing it down.

treaty (TREE-tee): An agreement between two groups of people saying that they will not fight each other and that they will try to help each other.

vomit (VOM-it): Vomiting or throwing up is your body's way of telling you that you are sick or that you have something poisonous in your stomach. You should never eat or drink anything that might be poisonous. If you ever feel like you need to vomit, don't try to hold it back. Your body knows what it needs to do.

West Indies (IN-dees): A group of islands south of Florida and east of Cuba. Columbus landed on these islands in 1492, thinking that he had found the East Indies, or Indonesia. When he saw Native Americans there, he called them "Indians" because he believed he was in Indonesia. Some of the islands in the West Indies are Puerto Rico, Hispañola, the Bahamas, the Greater Antilles, and the Lesser Antilles.

Index

plants. *See* foods, from garden; foods, wild
   plants
plant uses. *See* clothes; foods, wild plants;
   medicines; tools, Timucua
Potano, 14, 92
pottery, 85–89, 105, 114–18

religion, Timucua, 96. *See also* Christianity

Saturiwa, 14, 25, 29, 92, 93
Seminoles, 111, 131, 132
shaman, 69
shell. *See* tools, Timucua
skeletons, 113–14
slavery, 106, 108
Spain, the Spanish, xi, 16, 18, 99–100,
   105–6, 108

tattoos, 30, 147
Tequesta, 14
Thimogona, 12
time line, 11, 89, 117
tools, European, 95, 105
tools, Timucua, 80–90
trash middens. *See* middens
treaties: Timucua with French, 100; Spain
   with England, 106

villages, 50–58, 107

war, 94, 100–101
weapons, 27, 47, 80–82, 84, 95
West Indies, xi, 9, 106, 148

yaupon holly. *See* black drink